Answer Engine Optimization (AEO): Mastering SEO for Voice and Direct Answers

Module 1: Introduction to Answer Engine Optimization (AEO)

Lesson 1: What is Answer Engine Optimization?

1. What is Answer Engine Optimization (AEO)?

Imagine you're sitting in your living room and have a question: "What's the tallest mountain in the world?" You ask aloud, and a little voice from your device—like Alexa or Siri—answers,

"The tallest mountain in the world is Mount Everest!" *Boom!* You didn't even have to type a thing. This is where Answer Engine Optimization (AEO) comes in!

Answer Engine Optimization (AEO) is all about making content easy for these "smart assistants" to find and deliver a direct answer. It's like training content to be super helpful, fast, and able to give people the best answers with just one question.

AEO goes beyond traditional SEO (Search Engine Optimization), which usually helps websites rank high in search engines, and instead focuses on giving quick, clear answers.

Example:

If someone asks, "What's the capital of France?" AEO makes sure the device quickly answers, "Paris." Just like how you don't want to wait forever for ice cream, people don't want to wait for answers either! ●

---

2. AEO vs. Traditional SEO

Traditional SEO is a bit like setting up a big, flashy sign outside a restaurant to attract people in. The idea is to bring lots of visitors to the website, show them lots of details, and keep them around for a while.

But AEO is more like a quick drive-thru. Instead of pulling people into a big website, AEO gives them the exact answer they're looking for *right away*.

SEO (Search Engine Optimization)	AEO (Answer Engine Optimization)
Aims to bring people to a website	Aims to give direct answers to questions
Often long-form content, like articles	Short, clear answers
Focuses on website ranking in search	Focuses on being featured in answer boxes

Example:

Let's say you want to know, "What are the health benefits of apples?" In traditional SEO, you might see a webpage titled *"10 Health Benefits of Apples You Need to Know!"* and read through it. In AEO, you might hear Siri say, "Apples can help with heart health and boost your immune system." Quick and direct!

💡 Pro Tip:
For AEO, think *concise and clear.* Make sure answers are short but packed with useful info!

---

3. Purpose of AEO: Delivering Quick, Direct Answers

In today's fast-paced world, people don't want to wait. AEO's goal is to make answers as immediate and precise as possible, like having a library in your pocket! Whether someone is driving, cooking, or just too busy to read a long article, AEO is there to give them what they need instantly.

When we ask a device like Alexa or Google Home, "How much water should I drink in a day?" we want a quick, useful answer like "8 cups for most adults." We don't need a whole article about the history of water consumption (although that would be pretty cool). AEO helps devices give people just the facts!

Example:

You're helping your friend bake cookies and ask, "Alexa, how much sugar for chocolate chip cookies?" Instead of listing recipes, Alexa says, "One cup of sugar." That's AEO working at its finest—no mess, no fuss, just the answer!

⬤ **AEO Joke:**
What's an AEO expert's favorite answer?
The one that's *direct* and *to the point*! ⬤

---

4. Platforms and Devices Benefiting from AEO

AEO isn't just about one search engine; it's used across many devices and platforms. Here are some of the most common ones where AEO helps make people's lives easier:

- **Google Assistant:** Google's voice assistant that works on smartphones, smart speakers, and even cars. When you ask, "Hey Google, what's the weather like today?" it's AEO that helps provide the answer.

- **Amazon Alexa:** Alexa works on Amazon Echo devices and is like a handy friend who knows a lot about everything. You can ask Alexa, "How many teaspoons in a tablespoon?" and get an instant answer, thanks to AEO.

- **Apple Siri:** Siri is Apple's voice assistant on iPhones, iPads, and Macs. If you say, "Hey Siri, tell me a joke!" Siri might tell you something funny (although maybe not hilarious) with the help of AEO. ●

- **Microsoft Cortana:** Even though it's less common, Cortana is Microsoft's digital assistant and can answer questions on some Windows computers.

These devices are like little "answer engines" because they're designed to give quick replies and info whenever we need it. Without AEO, these smart assistants would have to scroll through lots of data, wasting time trying to find what we want.

Example:

Imagine asking Google Assistant, "What's 5 times 7?" You don't need a math class; you need a quick answer! Thanks to AEO, Google Assistant will answer "35" right away.

⬤ **Device Joke:**
Why did Alexa go to school?
To be a little smarter than Siri! ⬤

💡 **Pro Tip:**
Focus on keywords people might actually ask, like "how," "what," "why," and "where" questions. Think like a person who needs a quick fact, and structure your content around that.

---

5. Why is AEO Important for Today's World?

With more than **30% of searches** now done by voice, people are becoming used to talking to their devices. By 2024, there were over **100 million smart speakers** in homes worldwide! This means the demand for AEO-friendly content is only going up.

People ask all kinds of questions, from "How do I tie a tie?" to "What's the best way to clean a kitchen?" AEO makes sure that the answers are easy to find. This means websites, businesses, and creators who want to be heard must start creating content that fits AEO guidelines. It's all about *being there* for the people who need answers, fast.

Example:

Let's say someone asks Alexa, "What time does the sunset in New York?" Alexa can answer within seconds because the information is set up perfectly with AEO.

● Joke:
What did the AEO expert say to the blog post?
"Keep it short—no one's got time for that!" ●

💡 Pro Tip:
Keep in mind that AEO works best with **structured data**—which is a fancy way of saying that content should be organized well. Use headings, lists, and easy-to-read formats to help devices "see" answers clearly.

In Summary:

- **AEO** is the science of helping devices like Google, Alexa, and Siri give quick, accurate answers to questions.
- It differs from traditional **SEO** by focusing on direct, short responses rather than lengthy articles.
- Platforms like **Google Assistant, Alexa, Siri,** and **Cortana** all benefit from AEO, providing people with instant information on the go.
- **AEO is on the rise**, with more voice searches happening each day.

● **Final Joke:**
Why was the AEO expert so good at quizzes?
Because they always had the *answers* ready! ●

Now you know what Answer Engine Optimization (AEO) is and why it's so cool! It's all about giving people what they need, right when they need it. So next time you ask your smart device a question, you'll know just how much work goes into getting that answer to you fast!

Lesson 2: How Answer Engines Work

Ever asked Siri, Google, or Alexa a question? When you do, they're not just searching—they're finding answers! In this lesson, we'll explore how these answer engines (like voice assistants and AI-driven search tools) work their magic to get you answers fast. We'll also dive into how structured data helps answer engines and how search engines like Google show answers in handy formats like *featured snippets* and *answer boxes.*

---

1. What are Answer Engines?

Answer engines are smart tools that don't just give you a list of websites like regular search engines—they try to answer your question right away! Imagine them as super helpful robots whose job is to find the best answer in seconds.

Example:
Let's say you ask, "How tall is the Eiffel Tower?"
Instead of giving you a list of links, an answer engine
would say, "The Eiffel Tower is 1,083 feet tall." Quick
and to the point!

AEO Joke:
Why did the search engine go to therapy? Because it
had *issues* finding itself! ●

Pro Tip 💡:
If you're ever trying to get an answer from a voice
assistant, be specific with your question. The clearer
you are, the more accurate your answer will be!

---

2. Technology Behind Answer Engines: Voice Assistants & AI-Driven Search

Answer engines use *AI (Artificial Intelligence)* and *NLP
(Natural Language Processing)* to understand and
respond to questions. NLP helps the machine
understand human language, so even if you ask,
"Who's the President of France?" or "Who leads
France?" it knows you mean the same thing.

How Voice Assistants Work

Voice assistants like Siri, Alexa, and Google Assistant need to "hear" and then "understand" our questions. They do this in three simple steps:

1. **Hearing the Question:** The voice assistant "listens" to you when you speak. This is done through a *microphone* that catches your voice.
2. **Understanding the Words:** It then uses NLP to understand what you mean. For example, "How's the weather?" would make the assistant think about weather data.
3. **Finding an Answer:** Finally, the voice assistant searches its sources and gives you the answer.

Example:
If you say, "Alexa, what's 5 times 7?" Alexa will do the math and say, "The answer is 35." It's like having a calculator right in your speaker!

---

3. Structured Data: The Key to AEO (Answer Engine Optimization)

For answer engines to quickly find what they need, content creators often use *structured data*. Structured data is like giving instructions to the search engine to help it understand a webpage's content better.

How Structured Data Works

Structured data is a bit like *labels on a box*. Imagine you're organizing a closet. If each box says "shoes" or "toys," it's easy to find what you're looking for. Structured data works the same way, giving tags like "recipe" or "author" so answer engines can quickly pick out the details.

Example:
When a recipe website adds structured data, it might include tags like "cooking time," "ingredients," or "servings." Now, when you ask, "How long to bake cookies?" Google can find the baking time and show it to you in the answer box without you needing to open the site.

AEO Joke:
Why did the structured data feel misunderstood? Because no one *marked it up*! ●

Pro Tip 🔦 :
Using structured data can help content show up in answer boxes and snippets, which can make it easier for people to find your answers.

---

4. How Search Engines Show Answers: Featured Snippets and Answer Boxes

When you type or ask a question, you may have seen a quick answer box at the top of Google's search results. This is called a *featured snippet* or *answer box*.

Types of Featured Snippets

1. **Paragraph Snippets** – These are short answers in a few sentences.
2. **List Snippets** – These show lists, like steps to follow or top tips.
3. **Table Snippets** – These show data in a table, which is helpful for comparing things.

Each type helps answer questions in a way that's easy to read and understand.

Example:
If you search, "How to make pancakes?" a list snippet
might show up with steps like "Mix ingredients, pour on
pan, flip after 2 minutes, etc." You get the full answer
without scrolling down!

Pro Tip 💡 :
If you're creating a website, adding structured data and
organizing your answers in paragraphs, lists, or tables
can increase your chances of showing up in a featured
snippet.

---

5. Why Answer Engines Matter for AEO

Answer engines are becoming more important
because people now prefer quick answers. This means
AEO (Answer Engine Optimization) is crucial. AEO is
about organizing your content in a way that helps
answer engines find it fast.

How to Optimize for AEO

- **Use Structured Data:** This is like adding directions to your content. Search engines love clear instructions.
- **Be Concise:** Answer engines prefer short, direct answers.
- **Include Popular Questions:** Think of questions people might ask and include them in your content. For example, a "FAQ" section is perfect for AEO.

Example:
If you run a pet website, a great FAQ might be, "How much should I feed my cat?" Answer engines could then use that answer in a snippet.

AEO Joke:
What did the featured snippet say to the search engine? "I'm on *top* of things!" ●

Pro Tip 🔦 :
Answer engines value accuracy and clarity. So, when writing content, make sure it's clear and well-organized.

6. Future of Answer Engines

Answer engines will only get smarter with time. Experts predict that soon, they might understand not just what we say, but also *how* we say it, adding more personal touches to answers.

Example:
If you're asking for a "fun fact about penguins," a future answer engine might find and add extra fun details, like how they waddle.

AEO Joke:
What's an answer engine's favorite song? "I Still Haven't Found What I'm Looking For" by U2 – except they usually do! ●

Summary

Let's recap! Answer engines are powered by AI and NLP, making it easy to answer questions quickly. By using structured data, content creators help these engines find information fast, which is great for featured snippets and answer boxes.

Answer engines are amazing because they make finding information super simple. And by understanding how they work, we can make our content easier to find!

Lesson 3: Why AEO is the Future of Search

Introduction to AEO: What is it?

AEO, or **Answer Engine Optimization**, is all about giving people fast, simple answers instead of making them scroll through tons of web pages. Imagine you're asking a question, and *boom*—you get the answer right away! No digging through websites or reading long articles. That's AEO at work.

Growing Use of Voice Search and Question-Based Queries

Voice Search Basics

More and more, people are asking their devices questions instead of typing them out. Why? Because talking is faster and easier! Imagine you're playing with LEGOs, and you want to know, "Who invented LEGOs?" With voice search, you just ask, "Hey Google, who invented LEGOs?" It instantly replies without needing to type or even look at the screen.

Here's some fun data:

- **71%** of people would rather use their voice to search instead of typing. That's a lot!📣
- By 2024, more than **50% of all searches** are expected to be done by voice!

Example

If you ask, "Why is the sky blue?" a search engine using AEO will pull the most accurate answer and tell it to you right away instead of just showing you a list of web pages. This is why AEO is becoming so popular—people want answers quickly and clearly.

AEO Joke ⚫: Why did the smartphone break up with voice search? Because it just *wouldn't stop asking questions*!

Pro Tip 💡: If you're creating content for AEO, make sure to answer questions in a conversational tone. It helps voice search tools like Siri and Alexa pick up your content faster!

Current Trends: AI and Voice Assistants in Daily Life

AI and Voice Assistants Everywhere

Today, it's common to see people talking to their phones, smart speakers, and even their cars. Devices like **Amazon Alexa, Google Assistant, and Apple's Siri** are designed to help with everyday questions and tasks. They're not only smart but also constantly learning to get better at giving answers.

Why AI is a Big Deal for AEO

AI, or Artificial Intelligence, makes AEO even smarter. Let's say you ask Alexa, "What's the weather like?" Alexa has to understand:

1. You're asking about *today's* weather, not tomorrow's.

2. You want the *weather where you are,* not in another city.

AI learns your preferences over time, like what types of questions you ask most, making it even better at providing quick answers.

Example

You ask, "Alexa, what's a fun fact about space?" Alexa knows to look for an interesting, kid-friendly fact, like "Did you know a day on Venus is longer than a year on Venus?" Isn't that cool?

AEO Joke ●: Why did Alexa start working out? To keep up with all those *heavy* questions!

Pro Tip ❢ : Keep your questions simple when using AI or voice search. The clearer the question, the better the answer!

Why Users Prefer Quick, Conversational Answers

Why "Fast and Easy" Matters

Most people are busy, so they want answers without spending extra time clicking and reading. If you ask Google or Siri something, they try to give you a response right away, rather than leading you to a long article.

That's exactly what AEO aims for—quick, conversational answers that satisfy your curiosity without a lot of fuss.

Data that Proves It

- Studies show **65% of people** prefer getting direct answers rather than scrolling through websites.
- **Voice assistants** are expected to be used by over **8 billion devices** by 2025—just two years away! This includes smartphones, smart speakers, and even TVs.

Example

Imagine you're studying for a science quiz and want to know, "How far is the sun from Earth?" Instead of reading a whole book, you just ask Siri, and she says, "The sun is about 93 million miles away from Earth." Simple, right?

AEO Joke ●: Why did Siri break up with Google? Because it was always bringing up old searches!

Pro Tip 💡 : If you're writing content for voice search, keep it clear, conversational, and to the point. Think of how you'd explain it to a friend.

The Future of AEO and How It Changes Our Search Habits

As technology grows, AEO will be everywhere, helping us with homework, recipes, fun facts, and anything else we can think to ask! With more people wanting quick answers, search engines are evolving to provide exactly that.

How to Prepare for AEO's Future

To be ready for AEO:

1. **Write in a natural, question-and-answer format**. Think about what people might ask and answer those questions in your content.

2. **Use easy language**. This isn't the time to be fancy—simplicity wins!
3. **Be accurate**. Giving correct answers is key; nobody wants incorrect information.

Example

Let's say you run a website about animals. Instead of just listing facts, create a page called "Questions About Animals" and answer questions like, "What's the fastest animal in the world?" and "Why do lions roar?"

AEO Joke ●: Why did the web page apply for a voice search job? Because it had all the *answers*!

Pro Tip ●: Always ask yourself, "Is this answer something I'd want to hear if I asked a question?" If not, make it shorter or more direct!

Summary

AEO is all about helping people find quick answers by using voice search and AI-powered tools. With so many people using voice search on their phones, smart speakers, and other gadgets, AEO will only get bigger and more important. So, if you're creating content, think about the questions people might ask and answer them simply!

By following these tips and examples, you'll be ready for the AEO future and know exactly why people love asking questions—and getting answers—so fast.

Module 2: Understanding User Intent in AEO

Lesson 1: Types of User Intent in AEO

Welcome to Module 2! In this lesson, we'll dig into something super important in AEO (Answer Engine Optimization): *user intent.*

It's like figuring out why people ask the questions they do and how we can give them the best answers. There are different reasons—or "intents"—behind every question. When we understand those intents, we can make our answers stand out!

What Is User Intent?

Imagine you're asking a question. Sometimes, you want to learn something new. Other times, you're ready to buy something. And sometimes, you just want directions to get somewhere. This is *user intent*—what you hope to achieve by asking a question.

In AEO, we work with three main types of user intent:

1. **Informational** (learning something)
2. **Transactional** (buying or taking an action)
3. **Navigational** (finding a specific place)

Each type impacts how we create answers so that search engines know we've got the best one!

---

1. Informational Intent

Informational intent is like when you're curious and want to know more about something. It's when people ask questions just to learn.

Example:
Imagine someone types "What is AEO?" into a search engine. They aren't ready to buy anything; they just want to learn what AEO is.

For AEO, we need to focus on giving clear, detailed answers to these informational questions. The goal is to be the answer that pops up in a search engine's featured snippet or voice assistant result.

Data Example
Did you know that **80% of all online searches** are informational? People just want answers! So, being the best answer to common questions is crucial.

AEO Joke:
Why did the website answer every question?
Because it wanted to be a *know-it-all*!

Pro Tip 💡 : When targeting informational intent, focus on *clarity*. Try to cover all parts of the question simply. Using bullet points or lists can help you rank in snippets.

2. Transactional Intent

Transactional intent means the user is ready to take action. They might want to buy something, sign up, or download. These users are looking for solutions, products, or services.

Example:
If someone types "buy SEO e-book" or "sign up for AEO course," they're ready to do something. For AEO, this is a golden opportunity to direct them to products or services.

How This Impacts AEO Strategies
For transactional queries, our job is to make it easy for users to take action. We should provide buttons or links that lead them to exactly what they want.

Data Example
Studies show that **over 10% of searches** have transactional intent. These searches lead to higher conversions since users are already looking to take action.

AEO Joke:
Why did the searcher cross the road?
To *buy* something on the other side!

Pro Tip 🔦 : Use phrases like "Buy Now," "Sign Up," or "Get Started" to signal transactional intent. It helps search engines know you have the answer for action-takers.

---

3. Navigational Intent

Navigational intent means the user wants to find a specific page or website. They know where they want to go—they just need help getting there!

Example:
When someone searches for "OpenAI website" or "ChatGPT login," they're using navigational intent. They know they want OpenAI's site but might need help finding it.

How This Impacts AEO Strategies
For navigational queries, the goal is to make sure your site appears as the top result for your brand name or

specific service page. If people look up your name, you want to be easy to find!

Data Example
Only **10% of searches** are navigational, but they are very important for brand visibility. People expect to find the exact link they're looking for quickly.

AEO Joke:
Why did the search engine go on a diet?
It wanted to *navigate* to a healthier ranking!

Pro Tip 🔦 : Include your brand name clearly in page titles and descriptions to make it easy for people (and search engines) to find you!

Why Understanding Intent Matters in AEO

When we understand user intent, we can tailor our content to meet each need. Especially for AEO, this means focusing on question-based queries. For example:

- **Informational queries**: "How does AEO work?" Here, you'd want to provide a solid, detailed answer.
- **Transactional queries**: "Best AEO course to buy." This is where you can offer a product or service.
- **Navigational queries**: "OpenAI website." You'd want your site to be easy to find and on top for brand searches.

Knowing these intents helps us make the content relevant, so search engines know exactly when to show it!

Pro Tip 💡 : Use keywords that signal each intent. Words like "what," "how," or "tips" signal informational intent, while "buy," "sign up," or "discount" often show transactional intent.

Putting It All Together with Examples

Let's look at a few examples to see how understanding intent can shape our AEO strategy.

1. **Informational Query Example**
   - **Question**: "How to improve AEO?"
   - **Answer Strategy**: Provide a helpful, simple guide with step-by-step instructions.
2. **Transactional Query Example**
   - **Question**: "Purchase AEO software"
   - **Answer Strategy**: Highlight benefits, include a call-to-action like "Get it Now," and link to the product.
3. **Navigational Query Example**
   - **Question**: "OpenAI AEO platform"
   - **Answer Strategy**: Ensure the brand or product page is optimized to appear at the top.

AEO Joke:
How do AEO pros stay calm?
They take it *query* easy!

Final Thoughts on User Intent and AEO

User intent guides us in crafting answers that best fit what users need. The better we understand these different types of intent, the better we can create answers that match, leading to better visibility in search engines and voice results.

In AEO, the secret to success is giving users exactly what they want, based on their intent. By tailoring our answers, we make it easier for search engines to serve our content as the best match for their questions.

Pro Tip 💡 : Regularly analyze your traffic to understand which intents drive the most visits and adjust your strategy based on that insight.

Key Takeaways

- **Informational Intent**: Answers should be clear and helpful.
- **Transactional Intent**: Make actions easy with clear links and CTAs.
- **Navigational Intent**: Ensure people can find you by using clear branding.

Each of these strategies helps you optimize for AEO by aligning with what people need and making it easy for them to find answers.

Lesson 2: How to Research and Analyze Intent for AEO

In this lesson, we'll explore how to make your content ready for Answer Engine Optimization (AEO)! With AEO, you're creating content that's quick and easy for search engines to answer, like when people ask Google or Alexa questions.

We'll dive into some cool tools and learn how to pick just the right words to match people's questions perfectly!

Table of Contents:

1. Understanding AEO and User Intent

AEO stands for **Answer Engine Optimization**. Unlike regular SEO, which aims to help your page rank high, AEO is all about **helping your content show up as direct answers** to specific questions people ask search engines. Imagine you're building your content so it can appear in Google's answer boxes (you know, that neat little section at the top with quick answers!).

Example:
Let's say someone types, "Why is the sky blue?" If your content directly answers this question in a clear and simple way, it's more likely to get picked up as the top answer. Just like if someone asks Alexa the same question, it should be easy for Alexa to pull from your content!

AEO Joke:
Why did the SEO specialist bring a ladder to the internet?
Because they wanted to reach the "answer box"!

Pro Tip 💡 :
Always think like the user! If your page is answering questions quickly and clearly, you're on the right track for AEO.

---

2. Using Tools to Find Common Questions

To understand what people are asking, you need to use some great tools. Here are three of the best:

- **Google Search Console**: This tool shows you **what questions people typed into Google** before they clicked on your site. Think of it as a peek into what's popular!
- **AnswerThePublic**: Enter a keyword, and it shows a giant list of **questions people are asking online** around that topic. Super cool, right?
- **BuzzSumo**: Want to see what's hot? BuzzSumo shows **trending questions and topics** so you know what's catching people's attention.

Example Walkthrough with Tools:
Let's say you run a blog about pet care, and you want to know what dog owners ask online. Here's how you'd do it:

1. **In Google Search Console**, check your traffic for keywords like "dog training" or "dog food." Look for any questions in the queries section, like "How to train my puppy?"
2. **On AnswerThePublic**, type "dog" or "dog care." It will show tons of questions, like "What should I feed my dog?" and "Why does my dog bark at night?"
3. **On BuzzSumo**, see if there's a trend on dog behavior or health questions. You might spot a popular question like "How do I calm an anxious dog?"

AEO Joke:
Why did the website ask Google a question?
Because it heard Google always has the answer!

Pro Tip 💡 :
Combining tools gives you a complete picture of what people want to know. Try starting with

AnswerThePublic, then confirming trends in BuzzSumo for the most popular questions.

---

3. Keyword Research with a Question Focus

When you do keyword research for AEO, you're looking for **questions people commonly ask**. This means using keywords that start with **how, why, what, when, and where**. These "question keywords" make your content more answer-friendly!

Step-by-Step Guide to Question Keyword Research:

1. **Start with a topic** (like "plant care").
2. **Use Google Keyword Planner** or a similar tool, but focus on finding **question phrases** rather than single words.
3. Look for phrases like "How often should I water my plant?" or "What plants need the least sunlight?"

Example:
For a gardening website, instead of a keyword like "plant care," you'd want to look for questions like "Why are my plants turning yellow?" or "What's the best soil for indoor plants?"

Data Insight:
According to studies, **70% of voice searches** are question-based. That's why question-focused keywords are essential for AEO!

AEO Joke:
Why did the keyword break up with the long tail? Because it wanted "instant answers" without all the extra words!

Pro Tip 🔦 :
Think of your keywords like questions people would ask a friend or an expert. Phrasing them naturally makes it easier for search engines to pick your content as an answer.

---

4. Identifying Patterns in User Questions

Now, let's take things a step further. Not only do you want the right questions, but it's also helpful to **notice patterns** in how people ask. This helps you structure your answers in a way that feels more natural to the reader or listener.

Steps for Spotting Patterns:

1. **Collect your questions** from Google Search Console, AnswerThePublic, or BuzzSumo.
2. **Look for common language or phrasing.** For example, do people ask "How to…" or "What's the best way to…" when searching about a topic?
3. **Identify keywords and synonyms** used frequently. If a lot of people ask, "What's the easiest way to…" it's a sign that many are looking for simple solutions.

Example:
Imagine a site about fitness. If you see a pattern in questions like "Best exercise for beginners" and "How to start a workout routine," you know that people want easy, beginner-friendly tips. So, create content that's simple and helpful!

AEO Joke:
How does a search engine answer questions?
With lots of "queries" and a few "puns"!

Pro Tip 💡:
Write in a friendly, conversational style. The easier your content is to read, the more likely it will rank as an answer.

---

5. Pro Tips for Acing AEO

Here are some additional tricks to make sure your content stands out in Answer Engine Optimization!

- **Be Concise and Direct**: Aim to answer questions in the first few sentences. Google loves quick answers.
- **Use Lists and Bullets**: Organizing information makes it easier for search engines and readers to digest.
- **Add a FAQ Section**: Include a "Frequently Asked Questions" part on your page to address common questions.

- **Test and Improve**: Use Google Search Console to see which questions bring in visitors. Update your content based on what's popular.

Example:
Let's say you run a baking website. If you see that "How to make bread softer" is a popular question, add a direct answer with a few quick tips in bullet points.

AEO Joke:
What's an AEO specialist's favorite place to eat?
The answer buffet!

Pro Tip 🔦 :
If possible, provide short answers at the beginning, then give more details further down. This way, you cater to both people looking for quick answers and those who want the full scoop.

Conclusion

Mastering AEO is all about **understanding what people are asking** and **making your answers clear,**

quick, and friendly. By using tools like Google Search Console, AnswerThePublic, and BuzzSumo, you can uncover the real questions people have. And by optimizing your content with concise answers and natural language, you make it easier for search engines to choose your content as the top answer.

With these techniques and a little humor along the way, you're well on your way to becoming an AEO superstar!

Final AEO Joke:
Why do content creators love AEO?
Because they get to answer questions all day—and finally, someone's listening! ●

Lesson 3: Mapping Content to User Intent

In this lesson, we'll talk about why matching content to user intent is important and explore the main types of user intent: informational, navigational, and transactional. We'll also dive into different content formats, like guides and FAQs, and how these formats can boost your content's success. Finally, you'll learn some simple tricks for making your content AEO-friendly (Answer Engine Optimization) to help it pop up at the top of search results.

---

1. Understanding User Intent

Before creating content, we need to understand *why* users are searching. This "why" is called *user intent*. Think of user intent as the reason behind every search. There are three main types of user intent:

1. **Informational** - When someone wants to learn something (e.g., "How to bake cookies")
2. **Navigational** - When someone is looking for a specific website or page (e.g., "YouTube login page")
3. **Transactional** - When someone wants to buy something (e.g., "Buy kids' baking set")

⬤ **AEO Joke:** Why did the content get promoted? Because it had *intent*-ions to be helpful!

Pro Tip: Matching the right content to user intent can help it rank better and satisfy readers quickly.

---

2. Structuring Content by Intent Type

Let's see how to structure content for each type of intent. The key is choosing the right format and adding specific information.

Informational Intent

When people want to *learn*, they usually look for guides, tutorials, or articles. For example, if they search "how to tie a shoelace," they expect clear, step-by-step instructions.

- **Format Ideas**:
    - **Guides or How-To Articles**: Write guides that break down each step. Use headings like "Step 1: Make a Loop" for easy reading.
    - **FAQs**: Create an FAQ section to quickly answer common questions.

Pro Tip: Adding pictures or videos to guides can make informational content even better because visuals help people understand faster!

Example: Informational Content

For a search like "how to make chocolate chip cookies," you could structure your content like this:

Title: *How to Make Chocolate Chip Cookies – A Simple Guide*

Introduction: Briefly describe the process.

Steps:

1. **Gather Ingredients** - List all the ingredients with measurements.
2. **Mix Ingredients** - Explain how to mix and combine.
3. **Bake and Enjoy** - Tell readers about the perfect baking time.

Tip Section: Add baking tips for soft or crispy cookies.

Why This Works:

This structure aligns with informational intent because it provides clear steps, making it easy for users to follow along.

Navigational Intent

When users want to find a specific page, they might be looking for something like "Nike homepage" or "school library hours." They don't want lots of information—just the link!

- **Format Ideas**:
    - **Short, Direct Answer**: Provide a clear link or a quick answer.
    - **Branded Content**: Use branded terms in your headings so search engines recognize it.

    💡 **Pro Tip:** Add easy-to-spot links at the top of the page. This gets users where they need to go, quickly.

Example: Navigational Content

For a search like "Log in to Instagram," you could structure the content like this:

Title: *Instagram Login Page*

Introduction: "Here's the link to log in to Instagram and access your profile."

Link: Place the Instagram login link right at the top.

Why This Works:

This structure gives the user exactly what they need without any extra info. It matches their navigational intent by being short and direct.

Transactional Intent

When users are ready to *buy*, they're looking for product pages or comparisons. Think about what details a shopper wants, like prices, product features, and reviews.

- **Format Ideas**:
    - **Product Pages**: Include product details, images, and "buy" buttons.
    - **Comparisons**: If someone's comparing options, create a comparison chart for easy viewing.

● **AEO Joke:** Why did the content make the sale? Because it was spot-on with user *in-tense*!

🔔 **Pro Tip:** Including a call-to-action (CTA) button like "Add to Cart" or "Shop Now" can help push readers to make a purchase.

Example: Transactional Content

For a search like "buy kids' baking set," your page could be structured as follows:

Title: *Best Kids' Baking Set for Sale – Safe and Fun!*

Product Details:

- **Features**: Describe the set and its safe materials.
- **Price**: Clearly show the price.
- **Images**: Include high-quality images of the product.

CTA: Add an "Add to Cart" button below the description.

Why This Works:

This layout caters to transactional intent by offering quick buying options. Shoppers can see what they're buying and have an easy path to checkout.

---

3. Choosing the Right Format for Success

The format of your content can influence how well it answers the user's intent. Here's a guide to different formats that work well with each intent type:

Intent	Best Format	Example
Informational	Guides, FAQs	"How to grow indoor plants"
Navigational	Short Answer, Links	"Twitter homepage"
Transactional	Product Pages, CTAs	"Buy electric scooter"

Formats like **listicles** (e.g., "Top 10...") work well for informational content. **Comparison charts** are great for transactional content, especially if users are deciding between multiple options.

💡 **Pro Tip:** Use lists, bullet points, and bold text to make important information stand out. This helps readers (and search engines) quickly find key details.

---

4. Creating AEO-Aligned Content

Answer Engine Optimization (AEO) means structuring content so it's easy for search engines to pull quick answers. When done right, your content can land in the "featured snippet," a box at the top of search results that directly answers questions.

Steps for AEO-Aligned Content

1. **Use Clear Headings** - Break up sections with simple headings like "What is AEO?" or "Why Use AEO?"
2. **Write Concise Answers** - Give short, direct answers at the beginning of sections.
3. **Add Lists and Tables** - Use these to organize information in a way search engines like.

● **AEO Joke:** Why did the content end up in the answer box? Because it knew all the right *questions*!

Example of AEO-Aligned Content

For a search like "benefits of indoor plants," structure your page like this:

Title: *Top Benefits of Indoor Plants*

Introduction: Briefly state that indoor plants improve air quality, reduce stress, and brighten spaces.

Sections:

1. **Improves Air Quality** - Short, clear paragraph.
2. **Reduces Stress** - Another simple, quick paragraph.
3. **Brightens Spaces** - Explain this in one sentence.

Bullet List: Summarize benefits in a quick list.

Why This Works:

Each section is concise, clear, and easy to read. This format helps search engines pull quick answers directly from your content.

💡 **Pro Tip:** Always keep answers at the top of each section, making it easy for search engines to find them.

---

5. Final Thoughts

Mapping content to user intent isn't just about adding the right words; it's about structuring each piece with the reader's goal in mind. By knowing what users are looking for—whether information, navigation, or a product—your content can provide a fast and satisfying answer.

⬤ **AEO Joke:** What do you call an intent-focused writer? A search *engine*-ius!

By following these tips and formats, your content will be ready to rank high and be user-friendly. Happy mapping!

Module 3: Creating Content for AEO

Lesson 1: Crafting Precise and Direct Answers

In this lesson, we'll explore how to create content that answers questions directly and concisely. This skill is essential for AEO (Answer Engine Optimization) so that your content works well with voice assistants like Siri, Alexa, and Google Assistant. Voice assistants love short, direct responses—they help users get information fast without extra details!

Why Precise Answers Matter for AEO

Imagine asking your voice assistant a question, and it goes on and on instead of giving you the answer quickly. That's frustrating, right? Voice assistants need quick, punchy answers. They usually only read the first 30-40 words, so every word has to count. Think of this like answering a friend's question in a single sentence—they're just looking for the answer, not a story!

Tips for Writing Short, Accurate Responses

Let's dive into some tips to make your answers direct and useful.

1. Start with the Answer

- **Always begin with the answer.** For instance, if someone asks, "What's the capital of France?" start by saying, "The capital of France is Paris." Simple and to the point!
- **Example**:
    - **Question**: "How do I boil an egg?"
    - **Direct Answer**: "To boil an egg, place it in boiling water for 9-12 minutes."
- **AEO Joke**:
    - Why did the voice assistant break up with the long-winded answer?

- Because it was tired of running in circles for a simple response! ●

2. Use Bullet Points for Clarity

- Bullet points are a great way to list steps or points clearly. They're easy to read and help voice assistants deliver information in a clear order.
- **Example**:
  - **Question**: "How do I start a vegetable garden?"
  - **Answer**:
    - Find a sunny spot.
    - Prepare the soil by removing weeds.
    - Plant seeds according to packet instructions.
    - Water daily and enjoy your garden!

3. Provide Quick Summaries

- Summarize the answer whenever possible. Think of it as giving the "gist" rather than all the details.

- **Example**:
  - **Question**: "What is a healthy breakfast?"
  - **Summary Answer**: "A healthy breakfast includes whole grains, protein, and fruits, like oatmeal with berries and nuts."
- **Pro Tip** 💡: Stick to *one-sentence answers* whenever you can. If a detailed answer is needed, split it into clear points instead of one big paragraph.

4. Stick to Commonly Used Words

- Keep it simple! Voice assistants understand simpler words more easily, and so do listeners.
- **Example**:
  - **Question**: "What's a good exercise routine?"
  - **Simple Answer**: "A balanced routine includes cardio, strength, and flexibility exercises, like jogging, weight lifting, and stretching."

Using Bullet Points, Lists, and Summaries for Voice Assistant Retrieval

Bullet points and lists are golden for AEO. They're like mini-maps for your content that make information easy to find and digest.

Why Lists and Bullet Points Work for Voice Assistants

- **Voice-friendly**: Bullet points allow for quick scanning by voice assistants.
- **Easier listening**: They break down content into bite-sized chunks.
  - **Example with a List**:
    - **Question**: "How do you make a smoothie?"
    - **List Answer**:
      - Add 1 cup of fruit (like bananas or berries).
      - Pour in 1 cup of milk or juice.
      - Blend until smooth. Enjoy!

Quick Summaries: Instant Solutions

Quick summaries are perfect for answers that have a little more detail but still need to stay concise. They deliver the main idea in a brief statement.

- **Example**:
  - **Question**: "What are the benefits of yoga?"
  - **Quick Summary**: "Yoga helps improve flexibility, strength, and relaxation."
- **AEO Joke**:
  - Why are summaries so good for AEO?
  - Because they always get straight to the 'point'! ●

Examples of Optimized Responses for Voice Answer Constraints

Let's look at a few common questions and see how to craft responses that are both brief and packed with useful info.

1. **Question**: "What's the tallest mountain in the world?"

- Optimized Response: "Mount Everest, standing at 29,032 feet, is the tallest mountain in the world."

2. Question: "How can I make a cake?"
   - Optimized Response:
     - Preheat your oven to 350°F.
     - Mix flour, sugar, eggs, and butter.
     - Pour into a pan and bake for 30 minutes.

3. Question: "What's a good way to relieve stress?"
   - Optimized Response: "Exercise, deep breathing, and spending time outdoors are great for relieving stress."

4. Question: "What are some popular Italian dishes?"
   - Optimized Response:
     - Pasta carbonara
     - Margherita pizza
     - Lasagna
     - Tiramisu
   - Pro Tip 🔦 : For complex questions, focus on the top 3-5 main points only. This gives listeners what they need without overwhelming them.

Using Data to Back Up Answers (Even for Quick Responses)

If you can include a fact or data point in a short answer, it makes your response more reliable.

- **Example**:
    - **Question**: "How much water should I drink daily?"
    - **Data-backed Answer**: "Most adults should drink about 8 cups (64 ounces) of water daily."
- **Question**: "Why is sleep important?"
    - **Data-backed Answer**: "Getting 7-9 hours of sleep helps improve memory, mood, and health."
- **AEO Joke**:
    - Why do voice assistants love data-backed answers?
    - Because they're statistically more reliable! ●

Final Touch: Keep It Friendly!

Voice assistants often read information in a neutral voice, but your content doesn't have to be boring. A friendly tone or simple, upbeat language can make even quick answers feel welcoming.

- **Example**:
    - **Question**: "What's a good morning routine?"
    - **Friendly Answer**: "Start with a big glass of water, a 10-minute stretch, and a healthy breakfast to kick off your day!"

Summary Checklist for AEO-Friendly Responses

1. **Begin with the direct answer**.
2. **Use bullet points and lists** for easy scanning.
3. **Summarize when possible** to keep it concise.
4. **Incorporate simple words** to keep it listener-friendly.
5. **Add data points** to make answers more authoritative.

○ **Pro Tip** 💡 : Test your responses by reading them aloud. If you can say it in one breath, it's perfect for a voice assistant!

Wrapping Up

Creating content for AEO is all about crafting short, to-the-point answers that help people get what they need instantly.

Think of it like being a friendly expert who can give answers in a flash! Following these tips will help your content rank higher for voice search and make it easier for people to access your information.

With these skills, you're ready to start crafting content that's perfect for voice search. Remember, whether it's an 8-year-old or a voice assistant, keeping answers short, clear, and accurate is always the best approach.

Lesson 2: Structuring Content for Featured Snippets

Welcome to Lesson 2 of our SEO e-book! Today, we'll explore **how to organize content to boost your chances of snagging a featured snippet** – those eye-catching answer boxes that sit right at the top of Google's search results! By structuring your content with simple headers, easy-to-read Q&A formats, and keyword-rich summaries, you'll be on the fast track to featured snippet stardom.

---

1. What Are Featured Snippets?

Featured snippets are short pieces of text that Google highlights at the top of the search results to answer a query. It's like a VIP answer section! There are different types of snippets, but here are the top three:

- **Paragraph Snippets** – Google shows a short paragraph from your page.
- **List Snippets** – A numbered or bulleted list that outlines steps or points.

- **Table Snippets** – Organized data, like comparing prices, products, or locations.

Featured snippets answer common questions in a **concise, structured way**, so users get quick info without clicking on a link. Being a "snippet" means keeping things short and sweet!

> **AEO Joke:** Why did the SEO expert break up with the featured snippet? Because it just kept giving short answers! ●

---

2. How to Organize Content for Snippet Success 🏆

Getting featured in snippets is about understanding Google's love for well-organized information. Here's how you can structure your content to catch its attention!

Use Concise Headers 🏷️

Google "reads" web pages in sections, and **headers (like H2, H3)** help it understand the main topics. These headers should include keywords related to the topic. Keep them simple and specific to what people search for.

Example: If you're writing about "How to Tie a Shoe," use headers like:

- H2: How to Tie a Shoe in Simple Steps
- H3: Step-by-Step Guide to Tying Shoes

These headers tell Google exactly what's in each section, making it easier to pull out answers.

> **Pro Tip** 💡 : Think of each header as a mini-title. Imagine a question someone might type into Google, and use that as your header!

Use Q&A Formats 🗣

People often search in question format, so structuring parts of your content in a **Q&A style** can work wonders. Google loves pulling from Q&A formats because they're direct answers!

Example Q&A Layout for a Featured Snippet:

- **Question:** What is the best way to tie a shoe?
- **Answer:** The best way to tie a shoe is to make an "X" with the laces, loop one lace through the hole, and pull tightly. This creates a knot that keeps your shoe secure.

This style is straightforward and perfect for quick snippets!

> **AEO Joke:** What's Google's favorite Q&A? The ones that are already answered! ●

Add Keyword-Rich Summaries ▉

End each main section with a **short summary** that contains your focus keywords. Google often uses these summaries as the snippet text.

Example Summary for "Benefits of Drinking Water": "Drinking water keeps you hydrated, helps digestion, and supports skin health. Doctors recommend drinking at least eight glasses a day."

Data Tip: According to a study by SEMrush, **70% of featured snippets** contain keywords in the exact order as the search query. So make sure your summary sounds natural but also includes keywords directly!

> **Pro Tip** 💡 : Place a summary at the beginning of your article too. This can act as a "hook" and make it easy for Google to grab it as a featured snippet.

---

3. Types of Snippet-Friendly Layouts 🔧

Your content's layout can make a big difference in whether or not it becomes a snippet. Here are the top layouts that have shown success:

Paragraph Format 📜

For questions that need a short answer, write **2-3 sentence paragraphs** directly answering the query.

Example for "What is SEO?": "SEO, or Search Engine Optimization, is the process of improving a website to make it rank higher on search engines. It involves using keywords, creating quality content, and optimizing website structure. A well-optimized site can attract more visitors!"

List Format

For "how-to" or list-style searches, use **bullet points** or **numbered steps** to break down the process.

Example for "How to Bake a Cake":

1. Preheat the oven to 350°F.
2. Mix flour, sugar, and eggs.
3. Pour the batter into a greased pan.
4. Bake for 30 minutes.

   AEO Joke: Why did the cake get featured on Google? It had all the right ingredients!

Table Format

For comparison-type searches (like prices or features), a table helps organize information for easy reading.

Example for "Laptop Comparison":

Laptop Model	Price	Battery Life	Screen Size
Model A	$500	8 hours	13 inches

Model B $700   10 hours   15 inches

> **Pro Tip** 💡 : If you're using a table, make
> sure it's clear and easy to read. This way,
> Google can pick it up more easily.

---

4. Case Studies of Snippet-Friendly Content ■

Let's look at some real-world examples of websites
that structured their content and successfully captured
a featured snippet.

Case Study 1: Recipe Site – "How to Make French Toast"

A popular recipe site created a list-style format with
each step numbered for clarity. It included keywords
like "How to make French Toast" in headers and
provided a summary at the beginning. Google picked
up the list format, and it now appears as a featured
snippet!

Takeaway: List-style answers for step-by-step processes perform well, especially when organized in numbered or bulleted lists.

Case Study 2: Health Blog – "Benefits of Walking Daily"

This health blog included a concise paragraph summarizing the top benefits of walking daily and formatted the rest in a bullet list. Each benefit (e.g., "Improves heart health") was bolded to make it easy for Google to read.

Takeaway: Combining a **short summary** with a **bulleted list** of points is effective for paragraph and list snippets.

---

5. Quick Tips for Featured Snippet Success

- **Use numbered lists or bullet points** whenever you can.
- **Answer common questions** people have about your topic.

- **Include your main keyword** in the first 100 words if possible.
- **Format your headers as questions** (e.g., "How does SEO work?").
- **Create a content summary** for each main section.

> **Pro Tip** 💡 : Before you write, search for your topic on Google and look at the current featured snippets. This can give you clues on what format and layout Google prefers.

Wrap-Up: Structuring Content for Featured Snippets ✸

Getting your content into a featured snippet can boost your visibility and authority online. By organizing your content with concise headers, Q&A formats, keyword summaries, and snippet-friendly layouts, you increase your chances of landing that top spot.

So remember – keep it simple, keep it organized, and of course, keep it keyword-rich!

AEO Joke: Why did the featured snippet become a celebrity? Because it was always in the spotlight! 🎉

Lesson 3: Writing Conversational Content for Voice Search

Ever wonder why voice assistants like Siri, Alexa, and Google seem so chatty? They're always ready to answer questions like, "What's the best pizza near me?" or "How tall is Mount Everest?"

With more people using voice search, it's important to know how to write content that sounds friendly, easy to understand, and natural. Let's dive into the fun world of conversational writing for voice search!

Why Conversational Content?

Imagine talking to a friend versus reading a textbook. When we talk to friends, we use simple words, ask questions, and sound casual. Voice search works in a similar way: people ask questions like they're talking to a person! This is why we need to write in a way that feels natural, as if we're having a conversation. If our content sounds stiff or overly formal, it won't match what people are looking for when they use voice search.

> **AEO Joke ⬤:** Why did the SEO content go to therapy? Because it had trouble finding its "voice"!

Using Conversational, Natural Language

To match voice search queries, let's focus on three easy tips for making our content sound conversational and approachable.

1. Write Like You Talk

When you write, imagine you're chatting with someone. Avoid big, complicated words, and instead, use language that anyone can understand—even an 8-year-old! Think about words you use daily and how you naturally phrase things.

Example:

Instead of saying: "Locate the top-rated local pizza establishments in your vicinity."

Say: "Where's the best pizza place near me?"

> **Pro Tip** 🔦 : *Pretend you're explaining something to a friend who's curious about the topic. This keeps your tone relaxed and friendly!*

2. Use Short Sentences and Simple Words

People using voice search want fast answers, so it's best to keep sentences short and easy to follow. Break down big ideas into smaller, bite-sized pieces. Simple words help everyone understand what you're saying without having to look up words in a dictionary.

Example:

Instead of saying: "Implementing comprehensive SEO strategies is essential for digital success."

Say: "Want to get found online? Use simple SEO tricks to help people find you."

Data Snapshot ■: *According to recent research, 71% of people using voice search say they find it easier to get information quickly through conversational content.*

> **Pro Tip** ❢ : *If you read a sentence out loud and it sounds too fancy or confusing, rewrite it! Your voice search readers will thank you.*

3. Add Some Personality

Using friendly language and a bit of humor makes your content more relatable and enjoyable. Voice search users like hearing content that sounds natural and not robotic. Try using fun expressions or light humor to keep things engaging.

Example:

Instead of saying: "Eating fruits and vegetables is beneficial to one's health."

Say: "Want to feel amazing? Munch on some fruits and veggies every day!"

AEO Joke ⬤: Why did the content writer bring a ladder to work? To reach new conversational heights!

Question-Style Language and Conversational Phrases

Since people often phrase voice searches as questions, writing in a question-based style can help match their queries better. Imagine you're a curious kid or someone looking for quick answers.

1. Answer the 5 W's and 1 H (Who, What, When, Where, Why, and How)

Most voice searches start with one of these question words. By using them in your content, you're more likely to match the style people use when searching. Ask and answer questions directly in your content to create a natural flow.

Example:

Question: "What's the best time to plant a garden?"

Answer: "The best time to plant a garden is in spring when the soil starts to warm up."

2. Start with "How Can I" or "Why Should I"

A lot of voice search queries begin with phrases like "How can I…" or "Why should I…" You can use these to create section headers or start paragraphs to make your content sound like you're directly answering a person's question.

Example:

Section Header: "How Can I Make My Dog Happy?"

Content: "To make your dog happy, spend quality time with them, play fetch, and give them treats (but not too many!)."

> **Pro Tip 🔦:** *Sprinkle questions throughout your content to encourage people to keep reading. It's like they're following a friendly Q&A!*

3. Use Regional Language Nuances for Local Voice Search Optimization

If you're targeting a specific area, consider using terms or phrases that people in that region use. Adding a bit of local flavor helps make your content more relatable for people searching in that area. Just don't overdo it, or it might sound forced.

Example:

If you're writing for a New York audience: "What's the best deli around here?"

If you're writing for a Southern U.S. audience: "Where can I find some good ol' BBQ nearby?"

Data Snapshot ■: *A study found that 46% of people use voice search to find local businesses daily, so including local language can boost your chances of showing up in results!*

> **AEO Joke ●:** How does a local pizza shop rank higher in voice search? By saucing up its content with local flavor!

Tips for Making Content Friendly for Voice Search

Here are a few quick tips to wrap it all up!

1. Focus on "Conversational Keywords"

Instead of just using one or two keywords, think about how people would say their search out loud. Long-tail keywords, which are phrases with three or more words, can match conversational queries better than single words.

Example:

Instead of just "dog food," try: "What's the best dog food for small dogs?"

2. Create an FAQ Section

Adding a Frequently Asked Questions (FAQ) section is a great way to cover lots of voice search queries in one spot. Try using different question formats so your content answers multiple types of voice search questions.

Example:

Q: How often should I water indoor plants?

A: Water indoor plants about once a week, but check if the soil is dry first!

> **Pro Tip** 💡 **:** *Put the most common questions you hear from your audience in the FAQ section. This way, your content will feel personalized and helpful!*

3. Be Direct and Concise

Keep your answers brief and get straight to the point. Voice search assistants usually read only the first sentence or two of your response, so make sure those first lines pack a punch!

Example:

Instead of: "To ensure optimal growth, water plants weekly, especially during dry seasons, to maintain sufficient soil moisture levels."

Try: "Water plants once a week to keep them healthy!"

AEO Joke ●: Why did the SEO content go on a diet? Because it wanted to keep things short and "suite" for voice search!

Wrapping It Up

To write content that shines in voice search, remember to sound conversational, keep things short, and sprinkle in some questions and local flavor. Imagine you're talking to a friend or answering a curious question—and keep it fun! Voice search users are looking for friendly, helpful answers, and by using these tips, you'll make it easy for them to find exactly what they need.

So, let's get chatting—your readers (and their voice assistants) will thank you!

Lesson 4: Using Structured Data and Schema Markup for AEO

Introduction: What is Structured Data and Schema Markup?

Imagine if you're writing a story about your favorite snack, pizza ◀. Now, if you want people to easily find your story, you might label it as "pizza guide" or "yummy food" so that readers who love pizza know to check it out. Structured data and schema markup work a bit like that! They're special codes that help search engines understand what a webpage is all about. This makes it easier for search engines to show your content as the answer to someone's question.

Why Do We Need Structured Data for AEO?

AEO stands for **Answer Engine Optimization**. Just like SEO helps people find websites, AEO makes it easier for search engines (or "answer engines") to find quick, clear answers to users' questions. When you add structured data to a page, it helps answer engines understand it better, so your page can pop up in featured snippets, FAQs, and other cool answer boxes at the top of search results.

> **AEO Joke ●:**
> Why did the website break up with its schema markup?
> It felt like it was always structured! ●

Types of Schema Markup for AEO

There are tons of schema types, but for AEO, some of the most popular ones are:

1. **FAQPage** – For pages with frequently asked questions.
2. **QAPage** – For question-and-answer content.
3. **HowTo** – For step-by-step guides, like recipes or DIY projects.

Let's look at each schema type and how they help make your content more visible!

1. FAQPage Schema

An FAQPage schema tells search engines that your page contains a list of questions and answers on a specific topic. It's super handy for answering popular questions that people often search for.

> **Example:**
> If your website has a page about how to care for puppies 🖤, adding FAQPage schema could help it appear when

someone searches for "How do I care for a new puppy?"

Here's what an FAQ schema snippet might look like:

json
Copy code
```json
{
  "@context": "https://schema.org",
  "@type": "FAQPage",
  "mainEntity": [
    {
      "@type": "Question",
      "name": "How often should I feed
my puppy?",
      "acceptedAnswer": {
        "@type": "Answer",
        "text": "Puppies should be fed
3-4 times a day."
      }
    },
    {
      "@type": "Question",
```

```
      "name": "When can I take my puppy
for a walk?",
      "acceptedAnswer": {
        "@type": "Answer",
        "text": "Most puppies can go for
a walk at 8 weeks, after their
vaccinations."
      }
    }
  ]
}
```

Pro Tip 🔦 : Adding FAQ schema is a
quick way to get your answers seen right
on search pages, especially if you have
great answers to common questions!

2. QAPage Schema

A QAPage schema is great if your page has a question
with one best answer, but users can submit other
answers too. Think of it like a "best answer" format.

Example:
If you have a page where people ask questions like "What's the best way to brush my dog's teeth?" and people vote on answers, QAPage schema can help search engines show the best answers.

QAPage schema snippet example:

json
Copy code

```json
{
  "@context": "https://schema.org",
  "@type": "QAPage",
  "mainEntity": {
    "@type": "Question",
    "name": "What's the best way to brush my dog's teeth?",
    "acceptedAnswer": {
      "@type": "Answer",
      "text": "Use a soft-bristled toothbrush and special dog toothpaste."
    }
  }
}
```

}

AEO Joke ⬤:
Why did the FAQ page and QAPage get
along so well?
They both had all the answers! ⬤

3. HowTo Schema

HowTo schema is perfect if you're sharing step-by-step
instructions, like how to build a birdhouse 🐦 or how to
make slime.

Example:
A "How to Bake a Cake" page could use
HowTo schema to show up when people
search for step-by-step baking
instructions.

HowTo schema snippet example:

json
Copy code

```json
{
    "@context": "https://schema.org",
```

```json
  "@type": "HowTo",
  "name": "How to Bake a Cake",
  "step": [
    {
      "@type": "HowToStep",
      "name": "Preheat oven",
      "text": "Set your oven to 350
degrees."
    },
    {
      "@type": "HowToStep",
      "name": "Mix ingredients",
      "text": "Combine flour, sugar,
eggs, and butter in a bowl."
    },
    {
      "@type": "HowToStep",
      "name": "Bake the cake",
      "text": "Pour the mixture into a
pan and bake for 30 minutes."
    }
  ]
```

}

> **Pro Tip** 💡 : Adding HowTo schema makes it easier for users to follow your steps directly from the search page, so they're more likely to click through to your website!

Step-by-Step Guide to Implementing Schema for AEO

Adding schema to a webpage may sound tricky, but with a few steps, it's actually pretty simple! You'll even get to test it to see if it's working.

Step 1: Choose the Right Schema Type

Pick a schema type that best describes the content. Remember:

- **FAQPage** for common questions and answers.
- **QAPage** for single questions with answers.
- **HowTo** for step-by-step guides.

Step 2: Add the Schema Markup Code

Use JSON-LD format (JavaScript Object Notation for Linked Data) for schema markup. It's easy to read and recommended by Google.

Step 3: Paste the Code on Your Webpage

Paste your JSON-LD code into the <head> or <body> section of your HTML.

Step 4: Test with Google's Structured Data Testing Tool

1. Go to Google's Structured Data Testing Tool.
2. Paste your URL or code snippet into the tool.
3. Click "Run Test" to see if there are any errors.

If it's good to go, your page is ready for AEO!

> **Pro Tip 💡 :** Testing your structured data is crucial! Errors can prevent answer engines from understanding your page correctly, so always check your code.

How Structured Data Impacts Answer Engine Results

By using structured data, your webpage has a better chance of showing up in search features like "Featured Snippets," "Rich Answers," or "People Also Ask" sections.

Example: The Impact of HowTo Schema on Answer Engines

Let's say you have a DIY website, and you add HowTo schema to your page on "How to Make a Birdhouse." When someone searches, "How do I build a birdhouse?", your page might show up at the top with step-by-step instructions directly in the search results.

Here's how it could look on Google:

Snippet Preview:

- Step 1: Cut the wood.
- Step 2: Assemble the base.
- Step 3: Attach the roof.

Wrapping Up

Structured data and schema markup might seem like "computer talk," but they make your content friendly to answer engines. With just a few steps, you can make it easier for people (and robots) to find exactly what they're looking for!

> **AEO Joke ●:**
> What did the structured data say to the webpage?
> "I've got you covered...in rich snippets!"

Module 4: Optimizing Technical Aspects for AEO

Lesson 1: Page Speed and Core Web Vitals

Introduction: Why Page Speed Matters for AEO

Imagine you're at a candy store, and you're super excited to get a chocolate bar. But when you arrive, the shopkeeper is taking ages to unlock the door. Frustrating, right?

That's exactly how people feel when a website takes too long to load! Page speed — how quickly a website loads — matters a lot, especially for Answer Engine Optimization (AEO).

A fast website keeps visitors happy and helps search engines, like Google, find the information they need to answer questions.

Example: Studies show that if a website takes more than 3 seconds to load, over 50% of people leave! Imagine half of a classroom leaving a lesson because it started a few minutes late — that's a big problem online too!

AEO Joke:
Why did the webpage break up with its hosting?
Because it *needed space* — and a faster pace! ●

What Are Core Web Vitals?

Core Web Vitals are three key measurements that tell us how good (or bad) a website's experience is. Think of them as three big checkboxes a website needs to fill to make everyone happy:

1. **Largest Contentful Paint (LCP):** This checks how quickly the main part of a website shows up.
2. **First Input Delay (FID):** This checks how fast a website responds when you click or tap on it.
3. **Cumulative Layout Shift (CLS):** This measures if parts of the page move around while loading.

Why Core Web Vitals Matter for AEO

When websites meet these Core Web Vitals, people stay longer because they're not annoyed by slow load times or buttons that don't work right away. Search engines prefer websites that offer a good experience, so AEO relies on great Core Web Vitals to improve your site's ranking.

Pro Tip 💡 : Think of Core Web Vitals as a "Report Card" for your website! Improving your score on each makes sure visitors (and search engines) love it.

Largest Contentful Paint (LCP): How Fast Is the Big Stuff?

LCP measures the loading speed of the most important part of your page — like a giant image or title that people see right away. Ideally, it should load in **2.5 seconds or less**.

Example: Let's say you visit a recipe website, and the main picture of the dish appears quickly. If that picture is slow to load, people might leave before they even read the recipe.

Data Fact: Google found that websites with an LCP under 2.5 seconds keep visitors around 24% longer than those with slow LCPs.

How to Improve LCP:

1. **Compress Images:** Use smaller image sizes without losing quality. Tools like TinyPNG can help.
2. **Use a Content Delivery Network (CDN):** This helps deliver website content faster by storing copies closer to the visitor.
3. **Minify Code:** Cutting down on unnecessary coding "fluff" (like extra spaces) makes your website faster.

AEO Joke:
Why did the image file go to the gym?
It wanted to get a little "lighter" for a speedy load! ⬤

First Input Delay (FID): Quick Reactions Count!

FID measures how long it takes a website to react when you try to click, tap, or type. It's like asking a question and waiting for an answer — the faster, the better! For a good FID, aim for **100 milliseconds or less** (that's super fast!).

Example: Imagine you're on a game site and want to start playing, but when you press the "Play" button, nothing happens for a few seconds. Annoying, right? This is what poor FID feels like to users.

Data Fact: Sites with fast FID have 20% more engagement — people click around more because they trust the site to work quickly.

How to Improve FID:

1. **Reduce JavaScript:** JavaScript is what makes a website interactive, but too much of it can slow things down. Keep it light!
2. **Lazy Loading:** This means loading only the parts of the page people are looking at right now, instead of everything all at once.

Pro Tip 🔦 : Lazy loading is like only bringing out the food you need for dinner instead of setting out everything at once. It saves space and time!

AEO Joke:
Why was the JavaScript always tired?
It couldn't *function* without a break! ●

Cumulative Layout Shift (CLS): Stop the Jumpy Pages!

CLS is all about stability. Ever had a page suddenly "jump" while loading, making you accidentally click the wrong thing? CLS aims to stop this by making sure everything stays in place.

Example: You're on a shopping website and go to click "Buy," but just as you do, the page shifts, and you click "View Cart" instead. Frustrating! Keeping a low CLS score prevents this from happening.

Data Fact: Pages with low CLS scores have much higher conversion rates because people aren't annoyed by unexpected shifts.

How to Improve CLS:

1. **Set Sizes for Images and Ads:** Specify how big images or ads will be, so they don't suddenly pop in and move everything around.
2. **Avoid Flashy Pop-ups:** Ads or pop-ups can throw things around on the screen, so keep them to a minimum.

Pro Tip 🍦 : CLS is like setting your lunchbox on a table instead of a wobbly chair — it keeps everything from spilling!

AEO Joke:
Why did the webpage hate surprises?
Because it couldn't stand all the shifting around! ●

Tools to Measure Core Web Vitals

To check how your website is doing on LCP, FID, and CLS, there are tools you can use:

1. **PageSpeed Insights:** Just type in your website's URL, and this tool shows you scores for each Core Web Vital along with suggestions to improve them.
2. **Google Search Console:** If your website is linked to Google, this console will tell you how each page is performing in terms of Core Web Vitals.
3. **Lighthouse:** A Chrome-based tool that gives you a full breakdown of your website's speed and performance.

Example: PageSpeed Insights might tell you your LCP is too high because of a large image. It'll suggest compressing the image to improve speed.

Pro Tip 💡 **:** Run these tools regularly to keep your website in top shape. Just like checking a car's oil, it keeps things running smoothly!

AEO Joke:
Why did the website get excited about Core Web Vitals?
Because it knew speed was *key* to success! ⬤

Wrap-Up: Boosting AEO with Speed and Stability

In the world of AEO, keeping your website fast and stable is crucial. By mastering Core Web Vitals like LCP, FID, and CLS, you're not only making visitors happy but also helping search engines see your site as a top choice to answer questions.

Key Takeaways:

- **LCP:** Load big stuff fast.
- **FID:** React quickly to clicks and taps.
- **CLS:** Keep things stable and avoid unexpected shifts.

Final Pro Tip 💡 : Treat Core Web Vitals as a fun challenge! Improving these scores might seem tough, but each small step makes your website faster and smoother, which is a big win for everyone, including search engines.

With these skills, you're on your way to making your website the MVP (Most Valuable Page) in AEO. Keep it speedy, keep it stable, and watch the visitors and search engines smile! ⬤

Lesson 2: Mobile Optimization and Voice Search

1. Why Mobile-First Design Matters for Voice and Answer Queries

Let's think about our phones. These days, everyone is on a mobile device, right? We check the weather, chat with friends, even do homework on them! Because of this, search engines like Google want to make sure websites look great and work well on phones. They call this "mobile-first design." And here's something interesting—many people now ask questions out loud to their phones instead of typing them in! This is where "voice search" comes in.

Imagine you're asking your phone, "What's the tallest mountain in the world?" If the website you're sent to isn't easy to read or navigate on a phone, it's not helpful. Mobile-first design ensures that everything looks good, no matter what device you're on.

Example Time!

Let's say you own a website about animals. A user might ask, "Hey Siri, what do pandas eat?" If your website's information on panda diets is easy to read and loads quickly, your page might pop up as the answer! If it's hard to read on mobile, though, the search engine might choose another page instead.

Did You Know?

About 70% of internet traffic is now on mobile devices! ● This is why mobile-first is such a big deal!

2. Techniques to Improve Mobile Accessibility

To make sure our website is mobile-friendly, we need to think about accessibility, which means making it easy for everyone to use. Here are a few tricks to improve mobile accessibility:

- **Adjust Font Size**: Text should be big enough to read without zooming in.
- **Simplify Navigation**: Fewer buttons and simpler menus make it easier to get around.
- **Use Touch-Friendly Buttons**: Buttons should be big enough for fingers to tap easily.
- **Images and Graphics**: Use images that load quickly so your site doesn't slow down.

Imagine going to a website where you have to keep zooming in and out, trying to click tiny buttons. Frustrating, right? This is why mobile accessibility is key.

Example Time!

Let's say your website is about toys. You have a page with the top 10 toys of the year, and each toy has a "Learn More" button. If these buttons are too small to tap, users might accidentally hit the wrong button or get frustrated. Making these buttons a little bigger helps your visitors (and your website's success)!

AEO Joke Alert! ●

Why did the website go to the doctor? Because it wasn't "mobile responsive!" ●

---

3. Testing Tools for Mobile Responsiveness

Okay, we've talked about what makes a site mobile-friendly. But how do we know if it's actually working on all mobile devices? There are tools for that! These tools help check if everything looks good and works well on phones and tablets.

Here are a few popular tools:

- **Google's Mobile-Friendly Test**: This is a free tool from Google that shows if your website is easy to use on mobile. It even gives you suggestions for improvement.
- **PageSpeed Insights**: This tool not only checks if your site loads quickly but also suggests ways to make it faster. Slow sites are a no-go on mobile!
- **BrowserStack**: Want to see how your website looks on different devices and browsers? BrowserStack lets you test this, so your site looks great on any screen!

Example Time!

Let's say you run a blog about space. You want to make sure that kids, adults, and teachers can read it easily on any device. By using Google's Mobile-Friendly Test, you can find out if your blog loads well on a phone. If not, you might see suggestions like "Increase font size" or "Make buttons easier to tap." Fix these, and your site becomes friendlier for everyone!

Pro Tip 💡

Using Google Analytics can help you see what devices people are using to visit your website. If you see a lot of mobile users, it's time to focus even more on mobile optimization!

Final Thoughts on Mobile Optimization and Voice Search

Mobile optimization and voice search go hand-in-hand for creating a super user-friendly website.

Whether people are clicking through links or asking Siri questions, making sure everything is easy to read and quick to load is the golden rule.

So next time you're building or updating a website, remember the key ideas: mobile-first design, accessibility, and testing tools.

AEO Joke Alert! ●

Why don't mobile-friendly websites ever get lost? Because they have *responsive* navigation! ●

Lesson 3: Site Structure and Content Organization for AEO Success

1. Organizing Site Architecture to Make Content Discoverable by Answer Engines

Why Does Site Architecture Matter?

Imagine walking into a library, but there's no sign or structure to guide you. Books are piled everywhere, and you can't find what you're looking for. That would be confusing, right? Now, think of your website like a library. **Site architecture** is like the library map that helps answer engines (like Google) and users find the content they're looking for—quickly and easily!

When we organize content clearly, search engines understand our site better and are more likely to show our pages when people search for answers. This is called **Answer Engine Optimization (AEO)**, where search engines act like "answer engines," delivering direct answers to users.

Example:
If you have a website about baking, a good site structure would be:

- **Home**
  - **Recipes**
    - Cakes
    - Cookies
    - Breads
  - **Baking Tips**
    - Ingredients
    - Techniques
    - Tools

By organizing it this way, answer engines can quickly navigate each section and understand what topics you cover.

AEO Joke ●
Q: Why did the search engine refuse to organize a messy website?
A: It didn't want to get "404 errors" on its reputation!

Pro Tip 🔦
Keep It Simple: A simple structure is key. Try to keep all important pages within **3 clicks** from your

homepage. This helps answer engines and visitors reach content quickly!

---

2. Using Internal Linking and Categories to Enhance Content Visibility

Why Internal Links Are Essential

Internal links are links within your site that connect one page to another. They act like pathways, helping answer engines find all your content. If you have a page about "Cake Baking Tips," you might link it to your "Chocolate Cake Recipe" page. This way, when search engines discover one page, they're more likely to find the other page through these links!

Internal links also help guide visitors to related content, keeping them on your site longer, which is great for user engagement and AEO.

Example:
Suppose your baking website has a page on "Easy Baking Techniques." Adding links within that page to articles on "Basic Baking Tools" or "How to Measure

Ingredients Accurately" makes it easier for both search engines and visitors to find them.

Pro Tip 🍋
Use Descriptive Link Text: Instead of saying "Click here," describe the link like this: **"Read our Easy Baking Techniques guide"**. This gives answer engines a clue about the content and helps users know where they're going.

AEO Joke ⬤
Q: What's an answer engine's favorite kind of relationship?
A: Internal linking—because it's all about *connections*!

Using Categories to Organize Content

Categories help organize similar content into groups. Think of them as chapters in a book, helping answer engines and users understand the themes on your site.

Example:
If you own a health blog, your categories might look like this:

- **Fitness**
- **Nutrition**
- **Mental Health**

When you publish new posts, assign them to a relevant category. This helps answer engines see that your content is structured and grouped in a meaningful way.

Pro Tip 💡
Avoid Overlapping Categories: Try not to create too many categories that are too similar. Instead, keep your categories unique, so it's clear where each piece of content belongs.

AEO Joke ⚫
Q: Why was the blog content feeling insecure?
A: It didn't know which category to belong to!

---

3. Importance of Clean URLs and Concise Titles for AEO

Clean URLs: Making Your Web Address Easy to Read

A **clean URL** is one that's simple and clearly shows what the page is about. Answer engines prefer URLs without extra symbols or long, confusing numbers. A clean URL makes it easier for users and answer engines to understand and remember.

Example:

- Bad URL:
  www.mybakingblog.com/1021?_=id/12
- Clean URL:
  www.mybakingblog.com/chocolate-cake-recipe

See the difference? The second URL is clear and tells both users and answer engines exactly what's on the page.

Pro Tip 💡
Use Hyphens in URLs: Use hyphens to separate words (like www.myblog.com/easy-baking-tips) rather than underscores or just mashing words together. It's clearer for answer engines and easier to read.

AEO Joke ●
Q: Why did the URL break up with its partner?
A: It was too messy and full of strange characters!

Concise Titles: Helping Answer Engines Quickly Understand Content

Titles are like signposts for answer engines, telling them what your page is about. A concise, clear title helps answer engines know what to expect on your page, which can improve your AEO. Plus, concise titles are more likely to catch people's eyes in search results!

Example:
Imagine you're writing a title for a blog post. Instead of saying, "Everything You Ever Wanted to Know About Chocolate Cake Recipe," try "Chocolate Cake Recipe: Easy and Delicious."

Pro Tip 💡
Use Keywords in Titles: If your page is about "Chocolate Cake Recipe," make sure those words

appear in the title. It tells answer engines exactly what the content covers.

AEO Joke ●
Q: How does an answer engine feel about long, rambling titles?
A: Like it's reading a novel when it just wanted a snack!

Wrapping It Up: Keep It Organized, Keep It Clear

Having a well-organized site structure helps answer engines discover your content faster, making it easier to rank. Internal links and categories guide users through your site smoothly, while clean URLs and concise titles make both visitors and answer engines happy.

Quick Recap:

1. **Organize Your Site Architecture**: Structure content for easy discovery.

2. **Use Internal Links and Categories**: Guide visitors and answer engines through related content.
3. **Clean URLs and Concise Titles**: Make sure your URLs are easy to read and your titles are clear and to the point.

With these tools, you're on the right path to making your site friendly for answer engines and users alike!

Module 5: Utilizing Structured Data and Schema for Answer Engine Optimization (AEO)

Lesson 1: Introduction to Schema Markup for Answer Engines

Welcome to our lesson on schema markup, where we're going to unlock the secrets of making our websites super easy for search engines to understand!

Answer engines (like Google) want to find answers quickly, so using something called *schema markup* helps them understand our content. This lesson will cover how schema works, which types are most useful, and how schema can help us get into those fancy "answer boxes" we see on search results. Ready? Let's dive in!

What is Schema Markup?

Schema markup is like a secret language for search engines. Imagine a superhero with a magnifying glass that lets answer engines zoom in on exactly what our content means.

Instead of just reading our words, schema tells the answer engine, "Hey, this is a recipe!" or "This is a Q&A!" That way, answer engines can show our content to people in helpful ways—sometimes even right on the search page.

Example:

If you have a "How-To" guide on baking cookies, schema tells Google, "This is a step-by-step guide to bake cookies." So, when someone searches "How to bake cookies," Google might show your guide in a special box at the top!

Pro Tip 💡 :

Using schema markup can make your content eligible for "rich results," which means it can stand out with stars, images, or even answer boxes right in search results. Talk about extra sparkle! ✨

AEO Joke ⬤:

Why did the answer engine bring schema to the party? Because it made everything *structured*!

Why Schema is Important for Answer Engines

Answer engines like Google use schema markup to answer questions faster. By understanding exactly what your page is about, answer engines can provide the most accurate answers.

Think of it like having a helper at the library who knows exactly where every book is located. With schema, answer engines can quickly pull up your "book" (or website content) for the right question.

Most Relevant Schema Types

Now that we know schema markup helps search engines understand our content better, let's talk about a few of the most popular types! These are super important for anyone looking to improve their Answer Engine Optimization (AEO).

1. FAQ (Frequently Asked Questions) Schema

FAQ schema helps search engines see questions and answers on a page. This type is great if you've created a list of common questions and answers about your topic. By marking them with FAQ schema, you make it easier for answer engines to pull your answers directly into search results.

Example:

On a page about *puppy care*, you might have FAQ questions like:

- "How often should I feed my puppy?"
- "What toys are safe for puppies?"

With FAQ schema, these questions could appear in search results, helping people get the answers they need right away!

Pro Tip 🦴:

FAQ schema can improve your visibility, especially for mobile searches. Many users just want a quick answer, and if your site provides it directly, they're more likely to click!

AEO Joke ⬤:

How does FAQ schema work out?
By lifting up questions and answers!

---

2. Q&A Schema

Q&A schema is like FAQ schema but a bit different. While FAQ schema is for single answers (like a teacher answering questions in class), Q&A schema works for pages where there are many different answers to a single question, like a forum or community page.

Example:

Imagine a community forum where someone asks, "What's the best way to learn guitar?" You might get many answers:

1. "Take online lessons."
2. "Watch YouTube videos."
3. "Practice with a friend."

Using Q&A schema lets answer engines recognize there are multiple answers and show this in search results.

Pro Tip 💡:

Q&A schema is ideal if your site has user-generated content or forum-style discussions. It can help your content stand out by showing it's a community-supported answer!

AEO Joke ●:

What did the Q&A schema say to the FAQ schema?
"I'm the life of the *forum*!"

---

3. How-To Schema

How-To schema is amazing for step-by-step guides. If you're teaching people how to do something, like baking a cake or fixing a bike, this schema will make your content super visible on answer engines.

Example:

Let's say you have a page titled "How to Make a Smoothie." With How-To schema, you can mark each step:

- Step 1: Add fruits to the blender.
- Step 2: Pour in some milk or juice.
- Step 3: Blend until smooth.

By using How-To schema, your steps might appear in an easy-to-read format on search results, showing the answer right away.

Pro Tip 💡 :

How-To schema is popular on mobile searches since people often need instructions on the go. Plus, answer engines love showing quick solutions, so this can be a game-changer!

AEO Joke ⬤:

Why did the How-To schema start a cooking class? Because it wanted to show everyone the *steps*!

How Schema Markup Directly Impacts Answer Results

When you use schema markup, you're more likely to show up in what we call "rich snippets" or "answer boxes." These are the extra-special boxes that appear at the top of search results, often with images, stars, or steps.

According to a study, websites that use schema markup can see a 30% increase in click-through rates.

It's like having a VIP pass to get more eyes on your content!

Example:

Imagine you've used How-To schema on a blog about "How to Train a Puppy." When people search for "puppy training," your guide could appear at the top with clear steps, drawing in more readers. Answer engines love this because it lets them deliver a quick answer without making the searcher dig through multiple websites.

Pro Tip 🔦:

Answer boxes and rich results don't just get more clicks—they help you stand out as an authority in your field. And the more people trust your site, the more often they'll come back for more answers!

AEO Joke ⚫:

Why did the answer box break up with the regular link? Because it found someone more *relevant*!

Let's Recap

Schema markup is the special code that helps answer engines understand what your website is about. When answer engines "see" this markup, they can pull your content into rich results, making it more likely to get noticed.

Here's a quick overview:

1. **FAQ Schema**: Perfect for answering frequently asked questions on a topic.
2. **Q&A Schema**: Great for forums where there are multiple answers to one question.
3. **How-To Schema**: Ideal for step-by-step guides, making instructions clear and easy to follow.

Final Pro Tip 💡 :

Always test your schema markup with Google's Rich Results Test tool! This way, you can check if your schema is set up correctly before going live.

With schema, you're not just writing for humans but also giving answer engines the clues they need to understand your content. So, next time you're creating or updating a webpage, think about adding schema. It might just be your ticket to the top of search results!

Lesson 3: Leveraging Knowledge Graphs and Rich Snippets

Welcome to Lesson 3! In this chapter, we're going to learn about two superpowers of SEO—**Knowledge Graphs** and **Rich Snippets**. Imagine Google is like a superhero with an amazing tool belt, and these two tools make it super smart! They help Google understand, organize, and display content in ways that are super helpful for people. Let's dive in!

1. Importance of Knowledge Graph for Brand Authority and Search Visibility

What's a Knowledge Graph?
Imagine you have a friend who knows EVERYTHING. You could ask them anything—like "Who is the president?" or "Where is the Eiffel Tower?"—and they'd instantly have an answer.

Google's **Knowledge Graph** is like that friend! It's a giant database that helps Google understand people, places, and things and show quick answers in search results.

It's what makes that cool information box pop up on the right side of the screen when you search for something big, like a famous brand or a person.

Why It's Important for Brands
When your brand appears in Google's Knowledge Graph, it means Google sees it as important and trustworthy.

People will see your brand info right away, like a mini profile, making it easier for them to find what they're looking for.

This builds your **brand authority**, which is a fancy way of saying people can trust you. It also boosts **search visibility**, which means people find you more easily.

Example

Let's say you have a brand called "Fantastic Fitness." If Google sees your brand as an authority in fitness, it might show a Knowledge Graph box that says "Fantastic Fitness" with information about what you offer, your logo, and maybe some quick links to your website.

Imagine the number of people who'd check out Fantastic Fitness just by seeing that box!

AEO Joke ●

Why did the Knowledge Graph look so happy? Because it's full of "info" and "proud" of it!

Pro Tip 🔦

Make sure your website has an **"About" page** with all your important details—like what your brand does, its history, and why it's unique. This helps Google understand your brand better.

---

2. Tips for Optimizing Content to Increase Chances of Appearing in Google's Knowledge Graph

Getting into the Knowledge Graph isn't magic—it takes some **optimization**. But the good news? With a few clever moves, you can give your content a better shot at making it!

Tip 1: Use Clear, Factual Information
Google's Knowledge Graph loves facts, like "2 + 2 = 4." The more precise and clear your information is, the more Google can understand and trust it. Avoid jargon or tricky words; keep things simple and true!

Tip 2: Add Important Details
Include details about **who**, **what**, **where**, and **when** related to your content. For instance, if you're writing about Fantastic Fitness, make sure you include info about what services you offer, where you're located, and any special awards or recognitions you've earned.

Tip 3: Add Structured Data Markup
Structured data markup, also known as **schema**, is a special code that helps search engines read your content better. Think of it like adding labels to a grocery store so you can find things easily. When Google sees structured data, it says, "Ah! I know exactly what this is."

Example
Let's say you have a page about Fantastic Fitness.
You could use structured data to tell Google, "This is a
company page," "Our founder is Jane Smith," and "We
opened in 2020." Now Google's Knowledge Graph has
even more facts to share!

AEO Joke ⬤
Why did the content feel optimized? Because it was full
of "smart" data!

Pro Tip 🍦
Use a tool like **Google's Structured Data Markup
Helper**. It's like a cheat code for adding schema,
helping Google understand your website's info better.

---

3. Strategies for Obtaining Rich Snippets Using Structured Data

What's a Rich Snippet?
Rich snippets are like the "fancy" answers you see in
Google search results. They stand out because they're
extra helpful—showing ratings, prices, or lists. For

instance, if you search for a recipe, a rich snippet might show the recipe's ingredients or a star rating.

Rich snippets make your content look awesome and clickable! When people see rich snippets, they're more likely to click on them because they look unique and informative.

Example
Imagine you have a page on Fantastic Fitness with a workout guide. Normally, Google might just show the title and description, but if you add structured data, Google might turn it into a rich snippet with "Duration: 30 minutes" and "Difficulty: Beginner." People looking for a quick, easy workout will instantly know it's for them!

Strategies to Get Those Rich Snippets

- **1. Use FAQ Schema**: If you have a "Frequently Asked Questions" section on your page, add FAQ schema to it. This could help your questions and answers appear directly in search results!
- **2. Add Recipe Schema for Food-Related Content**: If your brand is related to food or

recipes, use recipe schema to show ingredients, cooking time, and ratings in search results.
- **3. Review Schema for Products**: Have a product page? Add review schema to show ratings and reviews. This makes your product stand out in search results, boosting the chances people click on it.

AEO Joke ●

How do rich snippets get rich? By earning all the clicks in Google's "click-bank!"

Pro Tip 🍭

Use **Google's Rich Results Test** tool. After you add structured data to your page, check it using this tool to see if Google recognizes it and is more likely to show it as a rich snippet.

Bonus Section: Fun Facts and Data

- **Did you know?** 30% of clicks go to rich snippets, especially when they offer extra info like images, prices, or reviews.

- **Data Insight:** Websites with structured data markup can increase click-through rates by as much as 20%!

Wrap-Up and Key Takeaways
Knowledge Graphs and rich snippets help Google display the most useful info for people, which means more people can see and trust your content. It takes a bit of effort, but the payoff is worth it—your content can look amazing in search results and attract more clicks!

Now that you've learned the basics, you're all set to make your content shine with the power of the Knowledge Graph and rich snippets. Keep these tips handy, and let's make Google show off your brand with a smile! ●

Module 6: Optimizing for Voice Search and Conversational AI

Lesson 1: Adapting to Natural Language Queries

Welcome to the world of voice search! Imagine you're asking a friend for directions, rather than typing it out. That's what voice search is all about—using our natural language to find information.

With voice search growing fast, this lesson will teach you how to adapt your content so it's easier for smart devices to understand.

---

1. Techniques for Phrasing Content Naturally to Match Spoken Questions

Voice searches are different from typing. When people type, they use short phrases like "best pizza near me." But when they speak, they're more likely to ask, "Where can I find the best pizza around here?" This means we need to adjust our writing to match how people speak.

Key Tips for Writing in a Natural Style:

1. **Write Like You Speak**
   Imagine explaining things to a friend. Instead of saying, "Location of top-rated pizzerias," you'd say, "Where can I find great pizza nearby?"
   Example:
   Instead of writing, "Optimal hydration methods for plants," try "How can I keep my plants hydrated?"

2. **Use Questions in Headers**
   Voice searches often start with "Who," "What," "When," "Where," "Why," or "How." Including these in headers helps search engines understand that your content answers a spoken question.
   Example:
   Header: "How does hydration help plants grow?"

Pro Tip 💡 : Start by thinking, "What would I ask if I wanted to know about this topic?" This approach can help you create more relatable content.

AEO Joke ⬤**:** Why did the smartphone apply for a job? It heard the boss was looking for a good "listener!"

---

2. Overview of Common Keywords and Phrases Used in Voice Queries

Did you know people use **70% longer phrases** when speaking than when typing? This is because voice searches use more **natural language**. To make content voice-friendly, we need to consider the types of keywords people say, like:

1. **Question Keywords:** Words like "how," "why," and "what" are more common in voice searches.
2. **Location Keywords:** Many voice searches are local, so phrases like "near me" or "in my area" are often used.
3. **Conversational Keywords:** These include phrases people would use in a conversation, like "I'm looking for..." or "Can you help me find..."

Examples of Adapting Keywords for Voice Search:

- Instead of "best coffee shop," try "Where can I find the best coffee shop near me?"
- Rather than "car maintenance tips," use "What are some easy car maintenance tips?"

Pro Tip 🎯 : Use a tool like **Answer the Public** to find out the exact questions people are asking about your topic.

AEO Joke ⬤: Why did the voice assistant break up with the keyboard? It found a better "connection!"

---

3. Examples of Adapting Content for Voice Recognition

When adapting content, make it straightforward. Here are some techniques to ensure voice search and conversational AI can easily understand and deliver your content:

1. **Use Complete Sentences**
   For instance, if someone asks, "How do I care for a cactus?" your content should say, "To care for a cactus, water it lightly every few weeks."

Example:
Instead of "Indoor plants care tips," write, "How can I take care of indoor plants?"

2. **Answer FAQs Directly**
Many voice searches are questions. Creating a Frequently Asked Questions (FAQ) section can help capture these searches. Each FAQ should provide a clear and concise answer.

Example FAQ Section:
- **Question:** "How often should I water my cactus?"
- **Answer:** "Water your cactus lightly every 2-4 weeks. It doesn't need much water because it stores moisture in its leaves."

3. **Use Short Paragraphs for Easy Recognition**
Long paragraphs can confuse voice search engines. By keeping sentences short and paragraphs bite-sized, it's easier for the AI to understand.

Pro Tip 💡 : Break down complicated answers into bullet points or numbered lists so that voice assistants can read the answer step-by-step.

AEO Joke ●**:** What did the content say to the voice assistant? "Are you reading me loud and clear?"

Putting It All Together

Adapted Example: Let's see how to optimize a section about "baking a cake" for voice search.

Original Text (Non-Voice-Friendly):

- "To bake a cake, gather ingredients. Preheat the oven. Mix ingredients in a bowl, pour into a baking tin, and bake at 350°F for 30 minutes."

Voice-Friendly Text:

- **Question**: "How do I bake a cake?"
- **Answer**: "To bake a cake, first gather all your ingredients. Preheat the oven to 350°F. Then, mix everything in a bowl and pour it into a baking tin. Finally, bake the cake for about 30 minutes."

The second version is direct and sounds like someone explaining it out loud, making it ideal for voice search results.

Quick Summary

To optimize content for voice search:

- **Think Like a Speaker:** Write as if you're talking to a friend.
- **Use Conversational Keywords:** Include words that match how people talk.
- **Focus on FAQ and Complete Sentences:** These are easier for voice recognition systems to understand.
- **Keep Answers Short and Sweet:** Voice assistants perform best with simple, direct answers.

Pro Tip 💡 : Test your content by reading it out loud. If it sounds too formal or complex, simplify it.

AEO Joke ⚫: How did the smartphone do in the voice search competition? It won by a "sound" margin!

By understanding natural language queries, you're setting yourself up to connect better with your audience through voice search. Good luck with your conversational journey!

Lesson 2: The Role of NLP (Natural Language Processing) in AEO

Welcome to another fun lesson in our SEO journey! Today, we're diving into a key part of making sure our content shows up in search results—especially voice search. And guess what? We're going to learn it in a way even an 8-year-old can understand!

What is NLP and How Does It Work?

NLP (Natural Language Processing) is a smart technology that helps search engines like Google understand human language. Imagine a robot trying to understand what we mean when we say, "Show me the best pizza near me!" It's not easy for robots, but NLP makes it possible by "teaching" them how we humans speak.

How NLP Helps Search Engines

NLP helps search engines understand:

- **What we mean** (our intent)
- **The context** (the "why" behind our search)
- **Related meanings** (connecting words that mean similar things)

For example, when we search for "best cheap pizza nearby," NLP helps Google understand:

- "Best" means high quality.
- "Cheap" means low price.
- "Nearby" means close to your location.

Without NLP, search engines would just look for pages with those exact words, which wouldn't work very well!

AEO Joke Alert ●
Why did the search engine break up with its keyword? Because it found the context!

Tips for Optimizing Content with Semantic Keywords and Context Clues

Alright, let's dive into some practical tips for using NLP to make your content shine in voice search results!

1. Use Semantic Keywords

Semantic keywords are words that are related to your main keyword. They add more meaning and make your content richer in context. For instance, if our main keyword is "pizza," we could use words like "cheese," "toppings," "pizzeria," and "delivery."

Example
Instead of just saying "cheap pizza," say, "Looking for an affordable pizza with delicious toppings? Find it here!"

2. Focus on Natural Language

When people use voice search, they often speak in full sentences, like asking a friend for advice. So, write your content as if you're talking to a friend.

Example
If you're targeting "how to make pizza at home," write: "Making pizza at home is fun and easy. First, get your ingredients ready..."

3. Answer Questions Directly

People using voice search usually ask questions, so it's helpful to include Q&A-style content. If someone asks, "How long does it take to bake a pizza?" and you have a clear answer, your content is more likely to be picked by search engines.

Example
Question: "How long does it take to bake a pizza?"
Answer: "Baking a pizza usually takes about 10-15 minutes, depending on your oven temperature and the thickness of the crust."

Pro Tip 💡
Add Q&A sections at the end of your articles to catch those common voice search queries.

AEO Joke Alert ⬤
Why did the search engine go to therapy?
Because it had trouble understanding "it's complicated!"

Examples of NLP-Enhanced Keywords for Improved Voice Ranking

NLP makes certain keywords more powerful because they're common in everyday speech. Let's look at some examples of how to optimize content for voice search with NLP-enhanced keywords.

1. Use Long-Tail Keywords

Long-tail keywords are longer, specific phrases people use in voice searches. Instead of "pizza recipe," someone might say, "How do I make a homemade pizza with cheese and pepperoni?"

Example
Title: "How to Make Homemade Pizza with Cheese and Pepperoni"
This specific title captures voice search terms more naturally.

2. Try Conversational Phrases

Instead of "best Italian food," try something like "Where can I find the best Italian food near me?" because that's how people speak in voice search.

Example

"Craving Italian food? Here's how to find the best Italian dishes near you, no matter where you are."

3. Leverage Related Phrases and Synonyms

Adding related phrases helps search engines understand your content better. For example, if your page is about Italian food, use words like "pasta," "pizza," "olive oil," and "pasta sauce."

Example

Instead of saying, "Italian food is delicious," expand it to "Italian food, from pasta to pizza, is loved worldwide for its rich flavors and fresh ingredients."

Pro Tip 📍

Think like a voice searcher! Imagine you're asking your phone a question about your topic. The way you'd naturally ask is how you should write.

AEO Joke Alert ⬤

Why did the voice search say "I'm tired"?
Because people kept asking it to repeat the same question over and over again!

Putting It All Together: Optimizing for Voice Search Using NLP

Now let's summarize what we've learned:

1. **Think of Keywords as Topics, Not Just Words**
   Instead of stuffing your content with one keyword, create a topic-rich piece with related words and phrases.
2. **Use Natural Language**
   Write like you're talking to someone, and avoid robotic phrases. Voice search loves natural, friendly content.
3. **Include Q&A-Style Content**
   Direct answers to questions make your content perfect for voice search results.
4. **Focus on Specific Phrases**
   Instead of broad keywords, focus on long-tail keywords or conversational phrases people use in real life.

Why Does This Matter for SEO?

Voice search is on the rise, with more and more people using their devices to find answers hands-free. In fact, **by 2023, voice searches accounted for 30% of all web browsing**. When you make your content voice-search-friendly, it becomes more discoverable, meaning more people will find it.

When search engines like Google rank your content higher, it means more visibility, more clicks, and potentially more customers or readers. So, NLP isn't just a tech term—it's the key to making your content ready for the future of search!

Pro Tip 💡
To check if your content works well for voice search, try reading it out loud. If it sounds natural and answers questions directly, you're on the right track.

AEO Joke Alert ⚫
Why did the SEO expert talk to their computer?
They wanted to optimize their conversation for voice search!

By following these steps, you'll be setting your content up for success in a world where voice search is becoming more popular every day. Remember, the goal is to sound like a friend, not a robot. Make sure your content is easy to understand, direct, and answers real questions people ask.

And that's a wrap on our lesson about NLP and voice search optimization!

Lesson 3: Local SEO and Voice Search Optimization

Welcome to Lesson 3! In this chapter, we're diving into Local SEO and Voice Search Optimization. We'll learn how to get search engines to notice local businesses when people ask things like, "Where's the best pizza near me?"

Local SEO and Voice Search Optimization are like digital maps guiding people to the right places. Let's explore how this magic works and even toss in a joke or two for good measure!

---

1. Strategies to Capture Local Voice Traffic, Especially for "Near Me" Queries

Think about when someone says, "Hey Google, find the best bakery near me." That's a voice search, and it's super popular, especially on mobile devices and smart speakers. Businesses want to show up as the answer to these "near me" questions, so we'll focus on how to capture local voice traffic.

How to Get Found in "Near Me" Searches

People often search using phrases like:

- "Best dentist near me"
- "Pizza shop open now near me"
- "Cheap car repair near me"

To get your business noticed in these searches, your website needs to speak Google's language. This includes:

1. **Using Location Words**: Add the city, neighborhood, or any well-known landmarks on your website.

2. **Adding Conversational Keywords**: Use phrases like "best [service] near me" in your content.
3. **Using Structured Data (Schema Markup)**: Schema is code that helps search engines understand your website better. For example, a "dentist" schema can tell Google exactly what kind of business it is and where it's located.

Example Time:

If you own a coffee shop called "Joe's Java" in Seattle, you'd want your website to include phrases like:

- "Looking for a coffee shop near downtown Seattle? Joe's Java has you covered!"
- "Best coffee near me in Seattle? Try Joe's Java."

Pro Tip 💡:

Always make sure your address is easy to find on your website's homepage and footer. Don't make Google search for it!

AEO Joke 😂:

Why did the coffee shop become great at local SEO? Because it kept espresso-ing itself on Google!

---

2. How to Optimize Google My Business (GMB) and Location-Based Content

Google My Business, or GMB, is a free tool where you can list your business and get seen by local customers. If your GMB listing is optimized, your chances of showing up in local searches increase.

Steps to Optimize Your GMB Listing

1. **Fill Out All Information**: Make sure you add your business name, address, phone number, website, and hours. Don't leave anything blank!

2. **Choose the Right Categories**: If you're a dentist, you'd select categories like "Dental Office" or "Dentist." The more specific, the better!

3. **Add Photos**: Upload clear, attractive photos of your business. People like to see what the place looks like before they go!

4. **Encourage Customer Reviews**: Ask happy customers to leave a review. A lot of good reviews can boost your ranking in local searches.

5. **Update Regularly**: Keep your GMB profile up to date with new info, especially if you're hosting events or have holiday hours.

Example Time:

Imagine you run a bookstore called "Sunny Books" in Austin, Texas. Here's what you'd add:

- Business Name: Sunny Books
- Category: Bookstore, Local Bookshop
- Address: 123 Main St., Austin, TX
- Hours: Mon-Sat, 10 am - 7 pm

- Photos: Pictures of the storefront, shelves, and popular book sections.

Pro Tip 🔦 :

Use posts on GMB to announce special deals or events, like "Book Club Wednesdays" or "Author Meet-and-Greets." It's like social media just for local searchers!

AEO Joke ⚫ :

Why do SEOs love Google My Business? Because it's their *business* to be seen!

---

3. Creating Location-Based Content for Voice Search

Once you've set up your GMB, it's time to create content that appeals to local voice searches. This can include blog posts, FAQ pages, and location-specific service pages.

How to Write Location-Based Content

1. **Local Blog Posts**: Write posts about your city and how your business helps locals. For example, if you own a pet store in Miami, you could write, "Top 5 Parks in Miami to Walk Your Dog."
2. **Frequently Asked Questions (FAQ)**: FAQs make it easy for voice searchers to find you. Use questions like "Where can I find dog grooming near me?" and answer them directly.
3. **Service Area Pages**: If you serve multiple cities or neighborhoods, create a unique page for each location. For instance, if you're a plumber working in Austin, create pages like "Plumbing Services in South Austin" or "Leak Repairs in Downtown Austin."

Example Time:

Let's say you're a bakery in San Francisco. Your blog could feature:

- "Best Birthday Cake Designs for SF Kids"
- "Where to Find Gluten-Free Pastries in San Francisco"
- "Top Pastries Near Golden Gate Park"

Adding location keywords (like "San Francisco," "Golden Gate Park") helps your content rank better in local voice searches.

Pro Tip 💡:

Use natural language! Instead of stiff phrases like "Pastries in SF," try "What's the best bakery near Golden Gate?" Conversational language is key for voice search.

AEO Joke ⬤:

Why did the SEO expert make a local bakery page? Because they kneaded more local traffic!

---

4. Examples of AEO for Local Search

Answer Engine Optimization (AEO) means making your site easy for search engines to answer people's questions directly. AEO isn't just SEO with a fancy name; it's about providing clear, easy-to-read answers.

Ways to Use AEO in Local Search

1. **Structured Data**: Schema markup (as we mentioned) is super important for AEO because it tells search engines about your business in specific terms.
2. **Clear Contact Information**: Google can't recommend you if it doesn't know where you are! Add your address, phone number, and email.
3. **Easy-to-Answer Content**: Make content scannable and easy to answer. Bullets, FAQs, and short paragraphs work wonders here.

Example Time:

If you're a dentist in New York, add FAQs like:

- "Where can I find emergency dental services near me?"
- "What dental services are covered by insurance?"

When Google sees these types of questions on your page, it knows it's a good answer for voice queries.

Pro Tip 💡:

If you're ever unsure what local keywords to use, try saying them out loud as if you're asking Siri or Alexa. Whatever sounds natural will likely work well for voice search!

AEO Joke ⬤:

What's an SEO's favorite type of data? Structured, because it keeps their life organized and ranking high!

In Summary

Local SEO and Voice Search Optimization are like opening the doors of your business to everyone nearby with a smartphone. By using these strategies, you're telling search engines, "Hey, I'm right here! Send them my way!" With a Google My Business profile, location-specific content, and a focus on local keywords, you can make your business stand out in local voice searches.

And remember:

- **Use location keywords** so people know where you are.

- **Optimize your GMB** profile to look appealing.
- **Write conversational content** to sound more natural in voice searches.

By focusing on these tips, your business can be the answer to all those "near me" questions out there!

Module 7: Building Authority and Trustworthiness for AEO

Lesson 1: E-A-T (Expertise, Authority, Trustworthiness) Principles for AEO

Welcome to the exciting world of E-A-T! ⬢ No, it's not lunch time—E-A-T stands for *Expertise, Authority, and Trustworthiness*. These three pillars help search engines, like Google, understand which answers on the internet are the best and safest for users. If we want people (and search engines!) to believe in what we write, we need to follow the E-A-T principles.

1. Understanding E-A-T Principles for High-Quality Answer Optimization

When search engines are looking for the best answers, they use E-A-T to pick out the most reliable, expert answers. Here's what each letter in E-A-T stands for:

- **E = Expertise** 🎙: Expertise means showing that you know what you're talking about. Think about it like this: if you're looking for baking advice, would you trust a baker with years of experience or someone who's only baked one batch of cookies? Exactly!
- **A = Authority** 🎓: Authority is like being the teacher in the classroom—the one everyone listens to because they have the right knowledge and skills. If many other people and websites look to you for advice, that shows authority.
- **T = Trustworthiness** 🛡: Trustworthiness means people can feel safe believing your information. This is about giving accurate, honest, and safe advice.

Example: Imagine you're searching for tips on "keeping your pet fish healthy." Google will choose a site written by a fish care expert, supported by trusted animal care organizations (authority), and which has accurate, safe advice (trustworthiness).

AEO Joke ●: Why did the search engine become friends with the math teacher? Because they both knew how to "add" to E-A-T!

Pro Tip 🍖 : Make sure your content has accurate information and is written clearly—both people and search engines will appreciate that!

---

2. How to Demonstrate Expertise and Authority in Content to Build Trust

If you want search engines to see you as an expert, you need to show your knowledge and make people feel confident in what you're saying. Let's break it down!

a) Use Facts, Data, and Examples ■

Facts and data show that you've done your homework. Imagine telling someone, "Fish need clean water."

That's helpful, but if you say, "Experts recommend changing 25% of your fish tank's water each week to keep it healthy," it sounds much more knowledgeable, right?

Example: A site on pet care might say, "According to research, 60% of pet fish survive longer if their tanks are cleaned weekly." This sounds authoritative and helps build trust.

b) Show Off Your Experience or Knowledge 🎓

If you're a professional, sharing your qualifications helps people believe in you. If not, sharing insights you've learned over time or experiences you've had works too!

Example: If you're writing about hiking, you could share, "After 10 years of hiking in different terrains, I've learned that bringing enough water and wearing good shoes is key to enjoying any hike!"

c) Use Clear Language and Avoid Jargon 🗣

Writing simply and clearly is part of building trust. If you sound complicated, readers (and search engines)

might think your information isn't accessible to
everyone.

Example: Instead of saying, "Maintaining optimal
aqueous habitat conditions is essential for piscine
survival," you could say, "Keeping fish tanks clean and
water fresh helps fish live longer."

AEO Joke ●: Why was the search result so
confident? Because it had "fish" in expertise and was
"net" full of data!

Pro Tip 💡 : Add links to reliable sources or studies
whenever possible to strengthen your expertise and
authority!

---

3. Techniques to Build Authority with Links and References

One of the best ways to build authority in AEO is by
connecting with other trustworthy sites through links
and references. This is like hanging out with a good
crowd—if respected sites link to you or you link to
credible sources, you start to look more reliable.

a) Link to Trusted Sources 🌐

When you link to well-known, reliable sources, it shows that you're backing up what you say with trusted information. This could mean linking to government health sites, universities, or well-established organizations in your field.

Example: If you're writing about healthy foods, you could link to a research article from a university about the benefits of vegetables. "According to Harvard's School of Public Health, a diet rich in vegetables can reduce the risk of many diseases."

b) Build Relationships for Backlinks 🔗

If other websites link back to your site, it tells search engines that other people find you reliable and knowledgeable. You can reach out to trusted sites and offer to share their content if they'll do the same for you.

Example: If you own a blog about books, you could reach out to popular libraries or book clubs online, offering to review some of their recommended books in exchange for a link.

c) Cite Your Sources and Give Credit ✏️

Citing sources properly shows readers (and search engines) that you're fair and honest about where you get your information. This builds trust with both your audience and search engines.

Example: "According to the American Heart Association, adults should aim for 150 minutes of moderate exercise each week to stay healthy."

AEO Joke ⬤: Why did the link refuse to join the party? It didn't trust the "source"!

Pro Tip 💡 : Focus on getting links from websites that are trusted and related to your field. A health site linking to you is better for your health blog than a random unrelated link.

Putting It All Together: Becoming an E-A-T Superstar!

To build authority and trust, we need to create content that shows expertise, connects to trusted sites, and is written in a friendly, clear way. When search engines see your expertise, authority, and trustworthiness, they'll be more likely to recommend your content in answer boxes and featured snippets, which are those big answer boxes you sometimes see at the top of search results.

Here's a recap:

1. **Show your Expertise** by sharing accurate, specific, and detailed information.
2. **Demonstrate Authority** by linking to trusted sources and sharing your knowledge or experience.
3. **Build Trust** by keeping your language clear, citing sources, and being transparent.

If we keep these E-A-T principles in mind, we'll be on the fast track to becoming a trusted voice online.

Final AEO Joke ●: Why was the website so popular with search engines? It had a huge "appetite" for E-A-T principles!

Lesson 2: Crafting Authoritative and Credible Content

Imagine you're telling a story to your friends, and you want them to believe you. You'd probably include some facts, maybe mention where you heard it, or share details that prove it's true, right? That's exactly what creating authoritative and credible content is all about! This lesson will show you how to make content that people (and search engines!) trust.

Strategies for Creating Informative and Authoritative Content

When people search online, they want answers they can trust. Here's how to make sure your content fits the bill:

1. Use Clear and Accurate Information

- **Explain Topics Simply**: Write in a way that even an 8-year-old can understand! Simplifying doesn't mean dumbing down—it means making your ideas easy to grasp.

- **Example**: If you're writing about the water cycle, start by explaining how water evaporates, forms clouds, and rains down again in a way that's clear and correct.

AEO Joke ●: Why did the search engine get a sunburn? It couldn't resist those hot, reliable facts!

2. Show Proof with Data and Facts

- **Include Numbers**: Data, like "98% of people use their phones to search online," adds weight to your words.
- **Example**: If writing about recycling, mention that "recycling one ton of paper saves 17 trees." Adding such data makes your point stronger.

Pro Tip 🍷 : Double-check where your facts come from. Reliable sources, like well-known studies or official websites, boost credibility!

3. Share Expert Insights

- **Bring in Quotes**: Expert opinions make your content sound even more trustworthy.
- **Example**: If you're writing about healthy eating, a quote from a nutritionist adds authority. Like, "Dr. Green, a nutritionist, says, 'Eating fruits and vegetables can boost your immune system!'"

AEO Joke ●: Why did the content writer bring an expert to the party? To give their story more "cred-ibility!"

Examples of Using Citations, Data, and Expert Insights in Content

Using outside sources gives readers confidence that your content is well-researched. Here's how to do it effectively:

1. Citations - Where to Find Good Information

- **Use Trusted Sources**: Sites ending in .edu, .gov, or popular scientific websites are usually reliable.
- **Example**: If writing about space, citing NASA makes your content super credible. Mention, "According to NASA, our solar system has eight planets."

Pro Tip 🔦: Always give credit! Instead of saying, "Scientists say…," try, "According to a 2023 report by NASA…"

2. Data - Making Content More Persuasive

- **Use Statistics to Support Your Points**: Numbers help people visualize what you're saying.
- **Example**: Writing about sleep? "Studies show that people who get 8 hours of sleep are 20% more productive." Stats like these make your content feel solid.

AEO Joke ●: Why did the stat go to therapy? It felt *too* used! Stats are great but don't overdo it.

3. Expert Insights - Adding Value with Quotes

- **Reach Out if Possible**: Quoting actual experts if you can reach them makes content even stronger. Or look for expert quotes online (make sure they're trustworthy).
- **Example**: A quote like, "Dr. Sleep, a psychologist, says, 'Kids need good sleep to concentrate in school,'" makes your advice on sleep habits more compelling.

Pro Tip 🦴 : Always fact-check quotes to ensure accuracy. Using wrong information can make content lose its credibility.

Tips for Keeping Content Updated and Credible

Even credible content can lose value over time. Keeping it updated ensures it stays useful!

1. Update Old Facts and Stats

- **Use Trusted Sources**: Sites ending in .edu, .gov, or popular scientific websites are usually reliable.
- **Example**: If writing about space, citing NASA makes your content super credible. Mention, "According to NASA, our solar system has eight planets."

Pro Tip 💡 : Always give credit! Instead of saying, "Scientists say…," try, "According to a 2023 report by NASA…"

2. Data - Making Content More Persuasive

- **Use Statistics to Support Your Points**: Numbers help people visualize what you're saying.
- **Example**: Writing about sleep? "Studies show that people who get 8 hours of sleep are 20% more productive." Stats like these make your content feel solid.

AEO Joke ⚫: Why did the stat go to therapy? It felt *too* used! Stats are great but don't overdo it.

3. Expert Insights - Adding Value with Quotes

- **Reach Out if Possible**: Quoting actual experts if you can reach them makes content even stronger. Or look for expert quotes online (make sure they're trustworthy).
- **Example**: A quote like, "Dr. Sleep, a psychologist, says, 'Kids need good sleep to concentrate in school,'" makes your advice on sleep habits more compelling.

Pro Tip 📍 : Always fact-check quotes to ensure accuracy. Using wrong information can make content lose its credibility.

Tips for Keeping Content Updated and Credible

Even credible content can lose value over time. Keeping it updated ensures it stays useful!

1. Update Old Facts and Stats

- **Set a Schedule to Review Content**: Check your content every six months to see if new information is available.
- **Example**: Let's say you have a fact that says, "There are 7 billion people on Earth." Since this number changes, check if it's still accurate in a few months!

Pro Tip 💡 : Create a reminder on your calendar to review important content.

2. Refresh Examples and Outdated References

- **Use Examples Relevant to Today**: Keep your examples fresh. A smartphone from 2015 might not be relevant to readers in 2024!
- **Example**: If you're explaining social media, mentioning "TikTok" might be more relevant to kids today than "MySpace."

AEO Joke ●: Why did the old stat break up with the website? It just couldn't keep up with the times!

3. Make Use of Current Events and Trends

- **Link to New Studies or Findings**: If there's a new study that supports your point, include it! This shows you're staying up-to-date.
- **Example**: For content on climate change, mentioning a new weather pattern or recent climate summit makes it current.

Pro Tip 💡 : Adding new sections for recent trends can improve your rankings because search engines love fresh content!

Conclusion

Creating authoritative and credible content is like being the "go-to" friend for advice! By providing solid facts, expert insights, and keeping your content up-to-date, you'll make it valuable not only for readers but also for search engines that rank trustworthy information higher.

Final AEO Joke ⬤

Why did the reliable content always rank higher?
Because it had all the *write* stuff!

Lesson 3: Managing Reputation and User Reviews

Welcome to Lesson 3 on Managing Reputation and User Reviews! This lesson is all about the power of online reviews and how they can help answer engines (like Google) decide to trust and recommend a business. We'll learn why positive reviews are important, how to get good ones, and even how to handle the not-so-great ones. By the end, you'll be a pro at managing reviews and boosting your brand's reputation!

Section 1: Why Positive Reviews Matter

Imagine this: You're trying to pick a game, and you see two options. One has tons of good comments like "Best game ever!" while the other has none. Which one would you choose? The one with all the great reviews, right? That's because reviews help people (and answer engines) decide if something is worth trying!

1. **Trust in Reviews:** Just like you trust your friend's advice, answer engines trust reviews. When a business has a lot of good reviews, it signals to the engine, "Hey, people like this place!" This can help boost a website's rank because positive reviews show that people are happy with it.

2. **Visibility Boost:** Good reviews mean that more people are likely to click on your business if it shows up in a search. The more people click, the more popular the answer engine thinks your business is, making it more likely to show up again.

3. **Higher Conversions:** For businesses, good reviews often mean that people are more likely to make a purchase or sign up for a service. According to a study, 92% of customers hesitate to buy from a business with negative reviews.

Example: A pizza place with reviews like "Best crust ever!" and "Quick delivery!" is more likely to attract new customers than one with no reviews or a few negative ones.

AEO Joke: Why did the answer engine cross the road? To find the best-rated restaurant on the other side! ●

Section 2: Techniques for Encouraging and Managing Reviews

Getting people to leave reviews doesn't have to be tricky! There are some simple steps to encourage positive reviews while managing any that aren't as glowing. Let's look at some strategies:

1. **Ask Nicely:** Sometimes, all it takes is asking. Right after someone has a good experience, gently ask them to leave a review. Many people are happy to share their thoughts if they had a great time!

Example: After a successful dental visit, the dentist's office might send a friendly email saying, "We hope you loved your visit! If so, we'd appreciate your feedback on Google to help others find us!"

2. **Make It Easy:** Provide direct links to review sites or have a review station on your website. The easier it is for people to leave a review, the more likely they will!
   Example: A hotel might include a QR code on the checkout receipt that guests can scan to leave a quick review on their phones.

3. **Respond to Reviews (Good & Bad):** When you reply to reviews, it shows that you care about customer feedback. If a review is positive, thank the customer. If it's negative, apologize and offer a solution. This shows you're listening and working to improve.
   Pro Tip 💡 : Always keep responses positive.

Avoid arguing or sounding defensive, even if the review isn't fair.

4. **Offer Small Incentives:** Some businesses might offer a little reward, like a discount on the next purchase, to encourage people to leave a review. Just remember to follow platform rules, as some sites have guidelines against "paid" reviews.
   Example: A coffee shop might give customers 10% off their next drink if they leave a review on the shop's website.

AEO Joke: What did the coffee shop say to the bad review? "Espresso yourself – we're listening!" ●

Section 3: Case Studies on AEO Success through Reviews

Here are a couple of real-world examples showing how reviews helped businesses rank higher and gain more traffic.

Case Study 1: The Local Bakery with a Loyal Following

A bakery called *Sweet Treats* in a small town decided to focus on gathering positive reviews. They encouraged regular customers to leave feedback by placing signs by the checkout and adding a QR code to the receipts.

After three months:

- The bakery's review count doubled.
- Their average star rating went from 4.0 to 4.8.
- They ranked as the #1 bakery in the area on Google.

More customers started coming in, and *Sweet Treats* even saw an increase in orders from people who found them online. Reviews not only helped their answer engine ranking, but they also boosted customer trust and loyalty.

Pro Tip 💡 : Be patient! Gathering reviews takes time, but the payoff can be huge in terms of both ranking and new customers.

Case Study 2: The Home Repair Service with Personalized Responses

A home repair service, *Fix-It Right*, wanted to stand out from other companies by responding to each review personally. If someone said, "Great service!" they'd reply with, "Thanks, [Customer's Name]! We loved helping you with your project." For any negative reviews, they'd politely ask for more details and offer a solution.

After six months:

- *Fix-It Right* saw a 30% increase in new customer inquiries.
- Their customer satisfaction rating jumped to 4.7 stars.
- They were featured on local "Best Of" lists due to their positive online reputation.

Their personalized responses helped create a connection with customers and showed that they truly cared, boosting their reputation and search ranking.

AEO Joke: Why did Fix-It Right do so well on answer engines? Because they nailed it with their reviews! ●

Wrapping Up: Keep Those Reviews Rolling In!

Reviews are like little gems for any business online. They tell answer engines, "Hey, people like us!" and make it more likely that the business will show up in search results.

By encouraging happy customers to leave reviews and responding positively to all feedback, businesses can build a solid online reputation and attract more people.

Quick Review Checklist:

- **Encourage Reviews:** Ask after positive interactions and make it easy.
- **Respond Positively:** Thank those who leave good reviews and stay cool with the negative ones.

- **Learn from Feedback:** Each review can help improve the business and show customers you're always trying to do better.

  Pro Tip 💡 : Never ignore a review! Each one is a chance to make your business shine.

  AEO Joke: What did the business say to its reviews? "Thanks for the feedback — you're making us a star!" ★⬤

With these tips and examples, you're ready to make your brand shine online and turn those reviews into a powerful tool for building trust and visibility.

Module 8 - Measuring and Analyzing AEO Performance

Lesson 1: Key Metrics to Track for AEO Success

In this lesson, we'll talk about tracking our success in **Answer Engine Optimization (AEO)**. Think of AEO as a way to make your content so smart and friendly that search engines can use it to answer people's questions. But how do you know if your content is actually doing well? We need to look at metrics—which are like scores or stats in a game—to find out!

What Are AEO Metrics?

Metrics are numbers that show us if our content is working or not. Here's how it helps: imagine you're trying to learn how good your friend is at soccer.

You'd probably check how many goals they score, how fast they run, and how many times they keep the ball.

These numbers tell you how well they're doing in the game. For AEO, we look at things like **answer box appearances** and **voice search rankings** to see if search engines think our content is helpful!

Important Metrics to Track in AEO

Here are some key metrics to keep an eye on:

1. Answer Box Appearances

The **Answer Box**, also called **Position Zero**, is the top spot on Google where answers to questions are shown. When your content appears here, it means Google thinks you have the best answer to a question.

Example: If someone asks, "What's the capital of France?" and Google shows your page with "The capital of France is Paris" at the very top, you're in the Answer Box! This is like getting a gold star in school for having the best answer.

Why It's Important: Answer Box appearances mean your content is highly visible. The more people see your answer, the more likely they are to visit your website.

AEO Joke ●: Why did the content sit at the top of Google? Because it *answered* all the right questions!

Pro Tip 🍦 : To increase Answer Box chances, create content that answers questions in short, clear sentences and includes headers like "What is," "How to," or "Why does" before your answers.

2. Voice Search Rankings

Voice search is when people ask questions using their voice on devices like Siri, Alexa, or Google Assistant. When your content ranks high for voice searches, it means it's easy to read out loud, short, and answers questions directly.

Example: If someone asks, "How far is the moon?" and Alexa reads your content that says, "The moon is

238,855 miles away," congratulations—you're ranking well for voice search!

Why It's Important: Voice search is growing fast! More people use their voices to search, so being voice-search-friendly is a big win for AEO.

AEO Joke ●: Why don't search engines talk more? Because they don't want to *voice* their opinions!

Pro Tip 🍦 : Use short sentences (15-20 words) and write naturally. Think about how people speak when asking questions.

3. Engagement Rate

Engagement Rate shows how much people interact with your content. High engagement means people like what they see and stay on your page, while low engagement means they're leaving quickly.

Example: If someone clicks on your page to read "10 Fun Facts About Dolphins" and they spend a few minutes reading each fact, that's high engagement!

Why It's Important: The more people enjoy and interact with your content, the better it performs in

AEO. Search engines love content that people find helpful and interesting.

AEO Joke 😅: Why was the webpage so popular? Because it was *engaging*!

Pro Tip 💡 : Use images, lists, or fun facts to make your content interesting. Interactive or visual elements keep people engaged.

4. Query Clicks

Query Clicks show the number of times people click on your content after seeing it in search results. More clicks mean people find your answer appealing or relevant to their question.

Example: If someone searches for "best pizza toppings," and they see your article titled "Top 5 Tasty Pizza Toppings," and they click it, that's a query click. The more clicks, the better!

Why It's Important: Query clicks mean people are choosing your content over others. High clicks tell search engines that your content is popular and should rank higher.

AEO Joke ●: Why did the user click on the pizza page? Because they *crust-ed* it to have the best toppings!

Pro Tip 💡 : Use catchy, clear titles and descriptions to increase query clicks. If people know exactly what they're getting, they're more likely to click.

5. Bounce Rate

The **Bounce Rate** shows how many people leave your page quickly after arriving. A high bounce rate isn't great because it means people didn't find what they were looking for. A low bounce rate means people are staying on your page and reading more.

Example: If someone clicks on your page, looks around, and leaves in a few seconds, that's a "bounce." But if they stay and read your whole article, the bounce rate goes down, which is good!

Why It's Important: A lower bounce rate shows that people are finding your content useful and engaging. Search engines prefer pages with low bounce rates.

AEO Joke ●: Why did the user stay on the webpage? Because they found it *un-bounce-lievably* interesting!

Pro Tip 📍 : To reduce bounce rate, make sure your page is easy to navigate, loads fast, and provides clear answers.

How to Monitor AEO Metrics

There are helpful tools you can use to check these metrics:

1. **Google Search Console**: This free tool shows you which queries (questions) people use to find your content, how often they click on it, and if you have any Answer Box appearances.
2. **PageSpeed Insights**: Helps you check if your page loads fast (a fast page keeps people engaged).
3. **Analytics Tools**: Other analytics platforms like **Google Analytics** let you track bounce rate, engagement rate, and query clicks.

Example: Let's say you're running a website about dinosaur facts. You check Google Search Console and see your page appears in the Answer Box for "What did T-Rex eat?" You also notice high clicks for "How fast was T-Rex?" but a high bounce rate for "Where did T-Rex live?" This info helps you improve the page to keep people reading!

Summary: Track, Tweak, Triumph!

In AEO, tracking metrics is like having a roadmap. You get to see where you're doing well and where you can improve. By keeping an eye on **Answer Box appearances, voice search rankings, engagement rates, query clicks, and bounce rate**, you're all set to know if your AEO is a winner!

AEO Wrap-Up Joke ⚫: Why did the Answer Box get promoted? Because it always had the *answer* for everything!

Final Pro Tip 💡: Don't just check your metrics once! Make it a habit to track them regularly. This way, you'll know exactly how to keep improving your AEO game. Happy tracking!

Lesson 2: Tools for Tracking and Analyzing AEO Efforts

Just like how a treasure map helps pirates find hidden treasure, AEO (Answer Engine Optimization) tools help us find the treasure of top search results.

By using special tools, we can track how well our AEO strategies are working and even make them better. Today, we'll learn about three popular tools: Google Analytics, SEMrush, and RankRanger. Plus, we'll have fun with a few jokes and a pro tip along the way!

---

1. Google Analytics: Your Data Detective

What Is It?

Google Analytics is like a detective for your website! It collects tons of information about who's visiting your site, what they're looking at, and how they got there.

Why It's Great for AEO

When we're trying to answer questions that people might ask, we want to know which pages visitors like best. Google Analytics helps us figure out things like:

- Which pages get the most visits (Are people finding what they need?)
- How long people stay on each page (Is our content helpful and interesting?)
- What keywords people are using to find us (Do we have the right answers?)

Example:

Let's say you have a page about "how to brush your cat's teeth." Google Analytics might show you that people love this page and spend five whole minutes on it! That's a sign that people find your answers helpful.

AEO Joke:
Why did the website bring a detective to the party? Because it needed more "page views"! ●

Pro Tip ▼ :
Use the **"Behavior Flow"** report in Google Analytics to see which paths people take on your site. It's like tracking a treasure hunt – you can see if they land on a

page, then move to another, or leave quickly. This helps you know which pages need some AEO love!

---

2. SEMrush: Your Spy in the Digital World 👓

What Is It?

SEMrush is a powerful tool that acts like a spy, showing you what keywords are popular and what other sites are ranking for. It's a great way to get inspiration for how to create content that answers questions people are asking.

Why It's Great for AEO

With SEMrush, we can see:

- What keywords are trending (So we know the latest questions!)
- How we rank compared to competitors (Are they answering questions better?)
- Ideas for new content topics (So we're always answering fresh questions!)

Example:

Imagine you run a blog about space for kids, and you notice "fun facts about black holes" is trending. SEMrush can show you that this keyword is getting a lot of searches. You can then create a page answering questions about black holes, like "What would happen if you fell into a black hole?"

AEO Joke:
Why did the SEO expert cross the road?
To get more *traffic*! ●

Pro Tip 🔦:
Try SEMrush's **"Keyword Magic Tool"** to find all the questions related to a single topic. If you search for "healthy snacks," it will show you tons of related questions people ask, like "What are good snacks for school?" This helps you find exactly what people want answers to!

---

3. RankRanger: Tracking Your Ranking Journey 🏯

What Is It?

RankRanger is like a ranking rollercoaster tracker! It lets you know how your content is moving up or down in search results. This tool is perfect for AEO because it shows if your answers are getting closer to the top spots!

Why It's Great for AEO

RankRanger gives you insights like:

- Where each of your pages ranks for specific questions (Are we in the top 10?)
- How your rankings change over time (Are we climbing up the ranks?)
- Which pages perform best (What are we doing right?)

Example:

Suppose you wrote an article on "how to bake the perfect chocolate chip cookie." RankRanger could show you that, after two weeks, your article has moved up from the 20th spot to the 12th spot in Google. This shows that your content is getting closer to the top answers!

AEO Joke:
Why do AEO pages love rollercoasters?
Because they're all about *ups and downs* in rankings!

Pro Tip 💡:
Use the **"Rank Insights"** feature in RankRanger to
see what changes are affecting your rankings.
Sometimes, small tweaks like changing a headline or
adding a bit more detail to your answer can make a big
difference!

How to Analyze and Interpret AEO Data

Once we gather all this information, it's time to make
sense of it. Think of it like being a scientist who looks
at clues to make discoveries. Here's a simple way to
analyze AEO data:

1. **Check Your Top-Performing Pages:** Look at
   your best-performing pages and ask, "Why do
   people love these?" Maybe they're helpful or
   answer a popular question.
   Example: If you see that your "how to make

slime" page is super popular, you might add a few extra tips to keep visitors coming back.

2. **Identify Weak Spots:** Some pages may not be doing as well. Ask yourself, "Do these pages need better answers?" Maybe they need clearer language, or you could add images. **Example:** If your "benefits of recycling" page isn't getting much traffic, try adding some fun facts or a colorful infographic to make it more interesting!

3. **Look for Trends:** Are certain topics or questions becoming more popular over time? Pay attention to what people want to know right now. **Example:** If you notice a lot of searches about "how to save water," it might be worth creating more pages on eco-friendly topics to match that trend.

Pro Tip 💡 :
Regularly update your content based on what your AEO tools tell you! Fresh content that answers current questions keeps your pages relevant and helps you stay on top.

Bringing It All Together: Using the Right Tools for the Job

Let's recap how each of our tools plays a role in AEO:

- **Google Analytics** helps you understand what people love (or don't love) about your site, so you can improve answers and keep people coming back.
- **SEMrush** gives you a sneak peek at trending keywords and competitors, so you're always ahead in answering the latest questions.

- **RankRanger** shows you how your pages rank over time, giving you clues about what's working and what might need some tweaks.

A Quick Summary:

- **Google Analytics:** Tracks visitor behavior, shows popular pages, and reveals keywords.
- **SEMrush:** Finds trending keywords, shows competitors' strengths, and suggests new topics.
- **RankRanger:** Tracks page rankings, shows ranking changes over time, and highlights top pages.

Each tool is like a different kind of superhero in your AEO journey – together, they make sure your answers are always in the right place at the right time!

Final AEO Joke:
What did the website say to the AEO tools?
"I'm counting on you to keep me in *good ranks*! ●

Lesson 3: Optimizing Based on Data and Feedback

Alright, we're diving into the world of improving and fine-tuning our AEO game! Imagine you've created a super cool robot that answers questions about anything.

But sometimes, the robot might miss out on the best answers or take a bit too long to respond. How do you make it better? By collecting data (or facts) and listening to people's feedback (what they think about the answers).

In this lesson, we'll learn how to use that data and feedback to make our AEO strategy shine!

Let's dive in with fun examples, easy-to-follow tips, and yes, a few AEO jokes to keep us smiling! ●

Why Data and Feedback Matter in AEO

When we create content to rank on search engines, it's like answering questions in a big contest. The better our answers, the more likely our content will show up as the top response.

But how do we know if our content is really winning? **Data** and **feedback** help us understand this! Data shows us numbers, like how many people visited our content or clicked on it, while feedback tells us if people liked it or found it helpful.

Example:

Imagine you wrote an article on "How to make chocolate cake." Lots of people are searching for it, and it's ranking well on search engines. But one day, you check the feedback and notice that many people say, "The recipe needs more chocolate!" ◆

What do you do? You can update your recipe with extra chocolate! Now, more people are satisfied, and they're more likely to choose your article over others. That's how feedback helps improve your AEO!

AEO Joke:

Why did the AEO content get so many clicks?
Because it knew exactly what the audience "searched"
for! ●

Step 1: Analyzing Your AEO Data

To see how well our AEO content is performing, we
can look at data, which comes from tools that measure
clicks, impressions, and how long people stay on our
content. Here are a few important numbers (or
metrics) to check:

- **Click-Through Rate (CTR):** This shows how
  often people clicked on your answer when it
  appeared on the search page. A high CTR
  means people liked the title or question you
  answered.
- **Bounce Rate:** This tells you if people left your
  content quickly. If the bounce rate is high, it
  could mean they didn't find it helpful.
- **Engagement Time:** This measures how long
  people stayed on your page. The longer they
  stay, the more they're probably reading and
  liking your content!

Example:

Let's say you check your AEO data and find out that your "Best Morning Exercises" page has a low CTR, which means people aren't clicking on it much. You decide to change the title to something more exciting, like "5 Fun Morning Exercises to Boost Your Energy! ✷" After the change, your CTR improves, and more people are checking out your article.

Pro Tip 💡 :

Use tools like **Google Analytics** or **Search Console** to see this data easily. These tools show you which pages are doing great and which ones need a bit of love and care!

Step 2: Gathering Audience Feedback

Sometimes, data alone doesn't tell us everything. That's where **feedback** comes in. Feedback can be comments, ratings, reviews, or even direct messages from people. It's like a friend telling you, "Hey, I think you should add a little more to this part." Listening to feedback helps you know exactly what readers think about your content.

Ways to Get Feedback:

- **Comments and Reviews:** Look at what people say about your content in the comments or reviews.
- **Surveys and Polls:** Create a short survey to ask people if they found your content helpful.
- **Social Media:** Check what people say about your content when you share it on social platforms like Facebook or Twitter.

Example:

You wrote a guide on "Tips for Better Sleep," but some readers comment that they would love to know about foods that improve sleep. Based on this feedback, you add a section on "Sleep-Boosting Foods." Now, your content covers more questions, making it even better for AEO!

AEO Joke:

Why did the AEO article join social media?
It wanted to see how many people "liked" it! ●

Pro Tip 💡 :

Ask open-ended questions at the end of your articles like, "Did you find this helpful?" or "What else would you like to know?" This makes it easy for readers to share their thoughts!

Step 3: Testing Changes for Better AEO

Now that you've analyzed data and collected feedback, it's time to make some changes! This process is called **A/B testing**, where you try two different versions of your content and see which one does better.

How to A/B Test:

1. **Pick one thing to change** (e.g., headline, intro, or call-to-action).
2. **Create two versions** of your content with this change.

3. **Compare the results** to see which version gets better engagement, CTR, or positive feedback.

Example:

Let's say you have two titles for your article about summer smoothies:

- Option A: "5 Refreshing Summer Smoothies You'll Love"
- Option B: "Beat the Heat with These 5 Delicious Summer Smoothies!"

After testing, you find out that Option B got a higher CTR. So, you decide to keep that title because it's helping you reach more people!

AEO Joke:

What did the A/B test say to the AEO strategy?
"Let's give people two options—they love choices!" ●

Step 4: Updating Content Regularly

Search engines love fresh content! Even if you have a great answer, it's essential to keep it updated with the latest information. If new facts or tips become available, add them to your content. This shows search engines that your content is always current, helping you maintain a top spot.

Example:

If you wrote an article on "Top Apps for Healthy Eating" in 2022, by 2024, some apps may have changed or new apps might be more popular. Updating this list with the latest apps makes your content more relevant and useful.

Pro Tip 💡 :

Set a schedule to check your top-performing content every 6 months. This way, you can keep it fresh without starting from scratch!

Step 5: Using Structured Data for Better AEO

Structured data is like adding extra details for search engines to understand your content better. It's a special code that highlights key parts of your content, like lists, questions, and ratings.

Example:

Imagine you have a recipe page for "The Best Chocolate Cake." Adding structured data helps search engines know:

- The ingredients list 🔖
- The cooking time 🔒
- The ratings ⭐

This makes it easier for search engines to show your content in rich snippets (fancy search results with extra info), making people more likely to click on it.

Pro Tip 💡 :

Use **Google's Structured Data Markup Helper** to add structured data to your content. This can help boost your AEO without changing the content itself!

Summary: Keep Improving with Data and Feedback

Optimizing AEO based on data and feedback is like taking care of a garden—you water it, add fertilizer, and trim it from time to time to make it grow beautifully. By analyzing metrics, listening to feedback, testing new ideas, updating content, and adding structured data, you can keep your AEO strategy at its best!

Quick Recap:

- **Look at the data:** Use CTR, bounce rate, and engagement time to see what's working.
- **Gather feedback:** Listen to what people say about your content.
- **Test and change:** Try new titles or ideas to improve AEO performance.
- **Update often:** Keep your content fresh and relevant.
- **Add structured data:** Help search engines understand your content better.

AEO Joke: What did the data say to the feedback?
"We make the best team for top-notch AEO!" ●

Module 9: Advanced AEO Strategies

Lesson 1: Answering Complex Questions with Long-Form Content

Why Complex Questions Matter for AEO

Have you ever tried to look up something online, and the answer you got was too short or missed key details? When people have complicated questions, they want complete answers that leave no stone unturned. That's where Advanced Answer Engine Optimization (AEO) comes in!

With AEO, search engines like Google are designed to help people get those detailed, step-by-step answers without scrolling through tons of sites. And that's why we're here: to learn how to create **long-form content** (like guides or in-depth articles) that answers complex questions fully!

What's a "Complex Question" in AEO?

Complex questions aren't simple "yes" or "no" types. They're often multi-part questions with "how," "why," "step-by-step," or "guide" in them. Think of questions like:

- "How can I start my own vegetable garden step-by-step?"
- "What are the stages of a butterfly's life cycle in detail?"
- "How do I bake a cake from scratch?"

These questions require answers with **multiple steps** and **clear explanations** to satisfy a reader's curiosity. Our goal is to answer these questions so well that readers—and search engines—will love it!

Step 1: Understanding Your Audience's Needs

To write great long-form content, start by understanding what the reader wants. If someone asks, "How do I start a garden?", they're probably a beginner who needs all the details, not just "plant seeds in soil."

Example: Imagine a reader wants to know how to build a treehouse. They need a guide that covers tools, safety tips, choosing the right tree, and even decorating ideas.

Pro Tip 🔦 : Use search tools (like Google's "People Also Ask") to find out related questions. This will help you see what other information readers might want!

Step 2: Structuring Long-Form Content for AEO

Once you know what your reader wants, it's time to plan your content's structure. A clear structure not only makes it easy for readers to follow but also helps search engines understand your content.

Use Headings and Subheadings

Headings and subheadings are like road signs for your readers. They tell them, "Here's what's coming up next!" For AEO, these signs help search engines understand the main topics in your content, improving its chances to appear for specific queries.

Example: If you're explaining how to grow tomatoes, your structure might look like this:

1. Choosing the Right Tomato Seeds
2. Preparing the Soil
3. Planting Your Seeds
4. Caring for Growing Tomatoes
5. Harvesting Time!

List Out Steps for Multi-Step Processes

If your answer has multiple steps, make each step stand out. Numbering them can help guide readers and tell search engines this is a step-by-step process.

Pro Tip 💡 **:** Use bullet points or numbered lists to make steps clear and easy to read. This can improve the chances of appearing in featured snippets (those quick answers you see at the top of search results)!

Add Images, Diagrams, or Videos

Visuals are a fantastic way to help readers (and search engines) understand complex answers. Sometimes, it's easier to *see* how something works rather than read about it.

Example: If you're teaching how to tie a bowline knot, a diagram of each loop and pull makes it much easier for readers to follow along.

Step 3: Crafting Detailed Answers That Satisfy Complex Queries

Now that we've got a structure, let's dive into the content! When crafting long-form answers:

- **Explain each part clearly.**

- **Use examples** to show the reader what you mean.
- **Break down concepts** into simple, understandable parts.

Start with the Basics, Then Go Deeper

Think about a lesson plan. You don't want to overwhelm the reader right away, so start with the basics, then go into details as needed.

Example: If you're writing about "How to Build a Birdhouse," start with the materials list, then give step-by-step instructions, and finally add extra tips like painting and roof options.

AEO Joke ●: Why did the bird read the long-form article on birdhouses? Because it wanted the tweet-mentorship!

Include FAQs to Cover Related Questions

Frequently Asked Questions (FAQs) are a smart way to answer common questions related to the main topic. It helps readers who have specific follow-up questions, and search engines like seeing these related answers, too.

Example: For a guide on "Growing Vegetables," your FAQs could be:

- "Can I grow vegetables indoors?"
- "What's the best fertilizer for tomatoes?"
- "How much sunlight do different vegetables need?"

Pro Tip 💡 **:** Think of your FAQs as a "mini-guide" at the end of the article. It can add value for readers and boost your content's relevance in search results.

Step 4: Optimize for Readability and Engagement

Engaging content isn't just about being informative—it should be easy and enjoyable to read. Here are some tips:

Use Simple Language

You don't have to use fancy words to sound smart. Clear, simple words work best for all ages, including 8-year-olds and search engines!

Example: Instead of saying, "Germination commences when seeds undergo an absorption process," you could say, "Seeds start growing when they soak up water."

Add Fun Examples or Stories

People remember stories, so try to make your examples fun and relatable.

Example: When explaining how to grow a plant, you might say, "Think of it like taking care of a pet. Plants need water, food, and love—just like a puppy!"

Step 5: Data and Statistics to Support Your Content

Using numbers or facts can make your content more credible. Search engines see data as a sign of trustworthy information, which boosts your AEO ranking.

Example: When writing an article on recycling, you could add, "Did you know that recycling one ton of paper saves 17 trees and 7,000 gallons of water?"

AEO Joke ●: Why did the statistic go on a date with the article? Because it made it 10 times more interesting!

Pro Tip ❢ : Try to keep statistics recent (from the last few years) and link back to reliable sources. This not only improves credibility but also helps readers trust your content.

Wrapping Up with a Conclusion and Summary

After answering a complex question in detail, wrap up with a quick summary. A conclusion helps readers remember the main points and gives them a sense of accomplishment for making it to the end.

Example: "In this guide, you learned how to grow your own vegetable garden, step-by-step. Remember, gardening takes time and patience, but with the right care, your plants will thrive!"

Final Checklist for Answering Complex Questions with Long-Form Content

1. **Understand the Question**: Know the reader's needs and any related questions.
2. **Structure for AEO**: Use clear headings, lists, and visuals.
3. **Write Detailed, Easy-to-Understand Answers**: Go deep without being complicated.
4. **Optimize for Engagement**: Use simple language and examples.
5. **Add Data and Wrap-Up**: Use stats to boost credibility, and end with a summary.

AEO Joke ●: What did the long-form article say to the search engine? "I've got all the answers you need—just give me the spotlight!"

Bonus Pro Tip 💡: Keep It Fresh!

Long-form content doesn't stop working once it's published. Updating it regularly with new information, examples, and data helps it stay relevant to both readers and search engines.

With these steps, you're ready to create long-form content that not only answers complex questions but also ranks well in search engines. Get ready to be the go-to source for detailed, helpful answers on the web!

Lesson 2: Leveraging Video and Visual Content for AEO

Introduction to Video and Visual Content in AEO

In the world of Answer Engine Optimization (AEO), video and visuals are superstars! Imagine you're looking for an answer online – say, "How to tie a shoelace" or "What's the best way to bake a cake?" Sometimes, watching someone show you the answer is way easier than reading a big wall of text. That's why search engines, especially answer engines, love to display video content in search results, especially for *how-to* and *FAQ* (Frequently Asked Questions) answers.

When we make videos or add visual content, we're helping these answer engines understand and display the information better. So, let's dive into how to make the most out of videos and visuals in AEO!

Role of Video Content in AEO

Videos make it easy for people to quickly understand answers, especially when they're showing step-by-step actions. Imagine trying to explain how to tie a shoelace just with words—hard, right? But with a video, it's clear and quick. The same goes for things like setting up a tent, cooking a recipe, or fixing a bike chain.

Fun Fact ■

According to a survey, 90% of people say they watch videos to help them learn how to do things themselves (DIY). This means more people are using video to answer their questions every day.

Example: Let's say someone searches for "How to make slime." If there's a video showing the steps to make slime, answer engines like Google will likely show that video at the top of the page. People love clicking on these video results because it's easier to follow along with the visuals.

AEO Joke ●: Why did the video get promoted on the search engine? Because it *nailed* the answer!

Pro Tip 🍦 : Keep your videos short and sweet! The shorter and more direct they are, the more likely answer engines will pick them to show as quick answers.

Tips for Optimizing Video Titles

The title of your video is like the "first impression." It should clearly say what the video is about, and it's best if it matches what people might be searching for. For AEO, we want our titles to be clear, simple, and to the point.

Example Titles for Better AEO:

- Instead of "Let's Make Yummy Pancakes," try "How to Make Pancakes in 5 Minutes"
- Instead of "Tips for Painting," try "How to Paint a Wall Like a Pro"

By using clear and searchable titles, answer engines can understand what the video is about and show it when people ask related questions.

AEO Joke ●: Why did the title go to school? Because it wanted to be top of its *class* in search results!

Pro Tip 💡 : Use words like "How to," "Guide," or "Tips" in titles—these words make it clear the video is answering a question.

Captions and Subtitles for AEO

Captions and subtitles aren't just for people who can't listen to the video; they're also for answer engines! When you add captions, you're adding text that engines can "read." This helps them understand exactly what your video covers, so they can show it when it matches a user's question.

Example: Adding Captions

If your video is about "How to plant a sunflower," and the captions include phrases like "plant the seeds," "cover with soil," and "water daily," the answer engine will recognize these steps and understand your video better.

Fun Fact ■

Did you know that 85% of Facebook users watch videos with the sound off? Captions help them understand your content, even in silence!

AEO Joke ●: Why did the caption go viral? Because it had the *write* stuff!

Pro Tip 💡 : Use simple language in your captions. This way, both viewers and answer engines can easily understand and match it with the right questions.

Schema Markup for Video Content

Schema markup is a special code that helps search engines understand your content. When you add schema to your video, it's like adding a label that says, "Hey, this video is a how-to!" or "This video answers a question about cooking!" Schema tells the search engine what the video is about and what kind of answer it provides.

Types of Schema to Use

1. **VideoObject Schema**: This tells answer engines the basics of your video—like the title, description, and thumbnail image.
2. **HowTo Schema**: For videos that show steps, like "How to Change a Tire," you can use HowTo schema to list each step. This way, engines understand that your video gives a clear answer with steps.

Example: Adding HowTo Schema

If you have a video on "How to Bake Cookies," your schema can list each step: "Mix ingredients," "Bake at 350°F," and so on. Now, the answer engine knows each step in your video and can display it in search results for people looking for cookie recipes!

AEO Joke ●: Why did the schema become a teacher? Because it was great at *organizing* things for everyone!

Pro Tip 💡: Use a schema generator tool online—they make it easy to create and add schema to your video without needing to code.

Optimizing Thumbnails for Video Content

Thumbnails are like the cover of a book—they make people want to click! If you're using video to answer questions, having a thumbnail that clearly shows what the video is about will help people choose your video over others. A thumbnail with a happy face, a clear "how-to" image, or a graphic of what's in the video works wonders.

Example of Effective Thumbnails:

- For a "How to Make Pizza" video, a thumbnail showing a fresh pizza or someone putting toppings on a pizza grabs attention.

- For a "Tips for Watering Plants" video, a thumbnail with a hand holding a watering can over a plant is perfect.

AEO Joke ●: Why did the thumbnail apply for a job in marketing? Because it was great at getting people to *click!*

Pro Tip 🔦 : Use bright colors and a clear, close-up image. It'll help answer engines and people understand what your video is about instantly.

Video Placement and Embedding for AEO

Where you place and embed videos can affect how answer engines see them. Putting videos on a webpage with relevant text can make it easier for engines to understand the video's purpose. Embedding videos on pages with helpful information (like blog posts) means answer engines see the video as part of the answer to questions about that topic.

Example:

If you embed a video titled "How to Train a Puppy" on a page with tips for new puppy owners, answer engines know it's answering questions about puppy training. This can make it more likely to show up when someone asks, "How do I train my puppy?"

AEO Joke ●: Why did the video stay on the webpage? Because it *embedded* itself in the answer!

Pro Tip 🔦 : Place your video near relevant text to help answer engines understand the connection between the video and the topic.

Conclusion

Video content is like a superpower in AEO. By creating clear, helpful videos with good titles, captions, schema, and thumbnails, you're making it easier for answer engines to find and show your content to people with questions. Remember to keep it simple, follow these tips, and add a dash of creativity! Soon, your videos will be the go-to answers for everyone's questions.

Final AEO Joke ●: Why do answer engines love videos? Because they're full of answers that *move*!

Lesson 3: Future Trends in AEO and Voice Technology

In this chapter, we'll dive into the exciting future of Answer Engine Optimization (AEO) and Voice Technology. As more people start using voice search, smart assistants, and conversational AI, websites need to adapt to meet new demands. This lesson will cover emerging trends and show you how to prepare your content and site structure for the future of AEO. Let's make it fun, easy, and clear—so clear even an 8-year-old would say, "I got this!"

---

1. Emerging Trends in Voice Search and Conversational AI

Voice search is booming! People love asking Siri, Alexa, or Google things like, "What's the weather?" or

"How many stars are in the Milky Way?" By 2025, it's estimated that **almost 50% of all online searches will be voice-based**. This means sites must be ready for these conversational searches. Let's look at some major trends.

a. Natural Language Processing (NLP) Improvements

NLP allows machines to understand human language. When you ask a question, NLP helps AI understand what you're really asking and provides the best answer. For example, if you say, "Who's the best soccer player?" it figures out you're asking for popular athletes, not any random player.

- **Example**: If your website sells soccer gear, you could write, "This soccer ball is just like the one used by pro players like Lionel Messi."
- **AEO Joke**: Why did the voice assistant break up with the chatbot? Because it felt "misunderstood!" ●
- **Pro Tip** 💡 : Make content sound natural and use words people actually say. "Soccer players" might work better than "football athletes" if that's what most people say.

b. Context-Aware AI

With advances in context-aware AI, search engines now understand context, so they can answer multi-part questions more accurately. For example, if you say, "Where's the Eiffel Tower?" and follow up with, "How tall is it?" AI understands you're still talking about the Eiffel Tower!

- **Example**: If your site is about famous landmarks, have pages that link info together. A page on the Eiffel Tower could link to related facts like its height, history, and the best time to visit.
- **AEO Joke**: Why do smart assistants make great students? Because they "follow up" on every question! ●
- **Pro Tip** 💡 : Create sections within pages that cover related questions, making it easy for AI to find answers quickly.

---

2. Preparing Content for Future AEO Trends

As voice technology grows, so does the need for content that answers questions instantly and accurately. Here's how to optimize your content to be future-ready.

a. Use Conversational Keywords

When people type, they might say, "Best pizza NYC," but with voice search, they'll say, "Where can I find the best pizza in New York City?" That means keywords need to be more conversational.

- **Example**: Instead of just "pizza places," try "Where to find the best pizza in New York." This sounds like a natural question.
- **Data Insight**: Studies show that **70% of voice searches are conversational**, meaning people speak to search engines like they talk to friends.
- **AEO Joke**: Why did the AI get promoted? Because it knew how to keep the "conversation" going! ⚫
- **Pro Tip** 💡: Write down some common questions you'd ask about your topic, then use those as keywords in your content.

b. Focus on Featured Snippets

When you ask a voice assistant something, it often reads the "featured snippet"—the short answer box at the top of search results. Creating content that answers questions in a few sentences helps you get featured in these spots.

- **Example**: If you're writing about dinosaurs, start with a summary: "Dinosaurs were large reptiles that lived millions of years ago. The T. rex, for example, was a meat-eater and is one of the most famous dinosaurs."
- **Pro Tip** 💡 : Summarize key points in a few sentences, making it easy for AI to use them in voice responses.

---

3. Optimizing Site Architecture for Voice and AEO

Good site architecture means organizing your website in a way that's easy for AI to understand. Imagine if a robot had to read a treasure map; the clearer it is, the faster it can find the treasure!

a. Create an FAQ Page for Common Questions

A Frequently Asked Questions (FAQ) page is great for voice search because it answers questions in a Q&A format, perfect for voice assistants.

- **Example**: If you run a cooking site, include questions like, "What's the best way to cook pasta?" and "How long should you boil eggs?"
- **AEO Joke**: Why do websites love FAQ pages? Because they always have the answers! ●
- **Pro Tip** ●: Write questions just like people would ask them. Keep answers brief and to the point.

b. Structure Content with Schema Markup

Schema markup is a fancy way of telling search engines what each part of your content is about. It helps AI understand things like reviews, recipes, and even events. This markup makes it easier for voice assistants to grab your info when people ask related questions.

- **Example**: If your page has a recipe, use schema to mark up ingredients, cooking time, and steps. This helps AI quickly find and share your recipe with someone who asks, "How do I make spaghetti?"

- **Data Insight**: Sites using schema markup have **20% higher chances of showing up in voice search results**.
- **AEO Joke**: How did the website win the voice search competition? It had great "structure!" ●
- **Pro Tip** 💡 : Use tools like Google's Structured Data Markup Helper to add schema to your pages easily.

---

4. Keeping Up with Future Trends

Voice technology will continue to evolve, and staying updated is key. Voice assistants are learning new things every day, and so should we!

a. Regularly Update Content

As questions change, your answers should too! If your content is old or outdated, it might not make sense in new searches.

- **Example**: If you have a page on phone technology, keep updating it to reflect the latest models, features, and trends.
- **AEO Joke**: Why do web pages love getting updates? Because they don't want to be "left behind!" ●
- **Pro Tip** 💡 : Schedule content reviews every 3–6 months to see if any info needs updating to stay relevant.

b. Monitor AI and AEO Innovations

Voice tech is moving fast! Keep an eye on new developments, especially around how people use voice assistants. New tools, trends, and updates can change how AEO works.

- **Example**: Follow blogs, watch tutorials, or join online communities for the latest AEO and voice trends.
- **AEO Joke**: Why do SEO experts like keeping up with AI news? Because they always "follow the trends!" ●
- **Pro Tip** 💡 : Join forums and groups that discuss voice search trends to stay in the know.

Conclusion

Voice search and conversational AI are making big changes in how people find information. To prepare for these trends, focus on creating natural, conversational content that answers real questions. Keep your site organized with FAQ pages, schema markup, and updated content to stay future-proof. With these steps, your site will be ready to answer questions, no matter how people ask them.

Final AEO Joke: Why did the website start talking to itself? Because it wanted to "get better at conversation!" ●

Keep Learning! 🙏

www.ingramcontent.com/pod-product-compliance
Lightning Source LLC
LaVergne TN
LVHW051442050326
832903LV00030BD/3205

*9 7 9 8 3 4 6 0 3 5 4 5 9 *